TOP SCORE

STUDENT'S BOOK 1

PAUL KELLY

OXFORD

UNIVERSITY PRESS

Contents

Getting started

Vocabulary

Food

1 Do the food quiz.

1 Put these meals in the correct order: dinner, breakfast, lunch

breakfast … …

2 Write the names of the objects in the pictures a–f.

3 A person that works in a restaurant is a …
   a cooker.   b cook.
4 The machine in a kitchen is a …
   a cooker.   b cook.
5 A meal in a British restaurant has three …
   a plates.   b courses.
6 Put these courses in the correct order: main course, dessert, starter

starter … …

7 A vegetarian doesn't eat …
   a vegetables.
   b meat.

Home

2 Where do you do these things at home? Match the activities 1-8 with the places a-h.

1 Brush your teeth and have a shower.
2 Play sport or relax in the sun.
3 Leave your jacket, coat, bag etc. when you arrive.
4 Do your homework, send emails and sleep.
5 Use the toilet.
6 Have lunch or dinner with visitors.
7 Sit and talk, read or watch TV.
8 Cook and eat.

a garden
b kitchen
c bathroom
d bedroom
e toilet
f dining room
g hall
h sitting room

School

3 Match the school subjects with the text books 1–7.

maths   geography   history   computer studies
~~English~~   science   art

1 English

In town

4 Look at the places a–h in the picture and answer the questions.

Where do you go to …

1 buy medicine?
2 watch a film?
3 play sport?
4 buy fruit and vegetables?
5 buy a newspaper?
6 buy bread?
7 have a meal?
8 write emails?

Prepositions of time

5 Complete the sentences with the prepositions *in*, *on*, and *at*.

1 We start school … September.
2 We start school … 8.30 a.m. and we finish … 3.30 p.m.
3 I have geography classes … Mondays and Wednesdays.
4 I do my homework … the evening and I study … the weekend.
5 We have a maths exam … October 13th.
6 I go to extra English classes … Mondays.
7 When I've got school I go to bed … 10 p.m.
8 … Saturdays and Sundays I go to bed … midnight.
9 … Saturdays I play tennis … the morning. I have football practice … the afternoon.

Prepositions of place

6 Complete the sentences with the words in the box.

behind   in   in front of   next to   on   under

1 The book is … the desk.
2 The pen is … the book.
3 The desk is … the window.
4 The flowers are … the vase.
5 The computer is … the flowers.
6 The shoes are … the desk.

 WORKBOOK PAGE 3

Grammar

to be and *have got*

1 Look at the rules. Choose the correct answers.

A	The verb *to be* is *an irregular / a regular* verb.
B	We use *is / are* to make the third person singular form of the verb *to be*.
C	We use *not / don't* to make the negative form.

2 Complete the dialogue with the correct form of the verb *to be*.

Karen	Hi Laura. Are you at the gym?
Laura	Yes, I **1**… .
Karen	Oh good. I've got a question for you. **2**… the gym only for people who are very good at sport?
Laura	No, it **3**… . Why? Are you interested in volleyball?
Karen	No, I **4**… not. I'm interested in gymnastics.
Laura	Well, our school PE teacher, Mrs Manley, **5**… the gymnastics teacher here.
Karen	Fantastic. She **6**… good. And **7**… Marta and Gary with you?
Laura	No, they **8**… . They **9**… at the cinema. They only come to the gym on Saturdays.
Karen	OK, thanks. See you at school tomorrow!

3 Look at the rules and the example sentences.

> *Have got* is an irregular verb.
> With *he*, *she* and *it* the form of the verb is different.
> *I've got a brother. I haven't got a sister.*
> *She's got a brother. She hasn't got a sister.*

4 Use *have got* and the information in the table to complete the sentences.

	Adam	Graham	Lisa
wristbands	✓	✓	✓
MP3 player	✗	✗	✓
CDs	✓	✓	✓
a tennis racket	✓	✓	✗
DVDs	✓	✗	✓
computer games	✗	✓	✗

Adam, Graham and Lisa have got wristbands.

1 Lisa … a tennis racket.
2 Adam and Graham … MP3 players.
3 Adam and Lisa … DVDs.
4 Graham … computer games.
5 Graham … DVDs.
6 Adam, Graham and Lisa … CDs.
7 Lisa … an MP3 player.

5 Write questions for the answers.

Has she got a car? Yes, she's got a car.

1 … ? No, my best friend hasn't got a bike.
2 … ? Yes, I've got a computer in my bedroom.
3 … ? Yes, they've got a big garden.
4 … ? No, my brother hasn't got a mobile phone.
5 … ? Yes, I've got friends in New York.
6 … ? No, we haven't got an English exam today.

6 Complete the text with the correct forms of *to be* or *have got*.

We (1)… a maths exam this week. I (2) … interested in computers and science but maths (3) … (not) my best subject. My best friend Sara (4) … a genius at maths. Maths (5) … important for computers and she likes computer programming. She (6) … three computers at home! At school we (7) … a computer room and a school website. The room (8) … twenty computers but it (9) … (not) computer games. Sara and the computer studies teacher (10) … in the computer room every lunch break! They design the school website.

Pronouns and adjectives

7 Complete the table.

Subject pronoun	Possessive adjective	Possessive pronoun
(1) …	my	mine
you	(2) …	yours
he / she	his / her	(3) … / …
we	(4) …	ours
(5) …	their	theirs

8 Complete the text with subject pronouns.

Do you like sport? I love sport! (1) … play volleyball and my PE teacher, Mr Smith, has got an Olympic medal for volleyball. (2) … 's very good! My best friend, Mary, does gymnastics. (3) … does gymnastics classes at the gym. My other friends play basketball. (4) … are in the school team. At the weekends I often watch sport with my friends. (5) … all like football and basketball matches. When I'm at home (6) … watch sport on TV with my dad. My mum and brother don't watch it. (7) … say sport on TV is boring! What about you? Which sports do (8) … play?

9 Complete the sentences with possessive adjectives.

1 I cycle to school. … bike is a mountain bike.
2 My dad likes Italian food. … favourite food is pasta.
3 She likes reading. … favourite books are about famous people.
4 We've got a new car. … new car is great.
5 You study a lot. … exam results are very good.
6 They've got a new house. … new house has got a swimming pool.

10 Put the possessive adjectives and the possessive pronouns in the correct place.

1 That isn't … mobile. It's … . (mine / your)
2 These aren't … CDs. They're … . (their / ours)
3 Superman isn't … favourite film. It's … . (his / my)
4 It isn't … book. It's … . (yours / her)
5 It isn't … car. It's … . (our / theirs)
6 She phones … best friend every evening. Do you phone …? (yours / her)

Possessive 's

11 Read the rules and look at the examples.

> We use 's after a name or noun to talk about possession.
> *Kate's brother*
> We add ' after a plural noun ending in s.
> *My cousins' computer*

12 Use possessive 's to write about the people and their things.

Pete's CDs

1 The students / classroom
2 Our friends / house
3 The girl / bag
4 Naomi / bike
5 My uncle / car

there is / there are

13 Complete the sentences with *there is* and *there are*.

There is an MP3 player on the bed.

1 … some flowers on the cupboard.
2 … a magazine on the floor.
3 … some books on the shelf.
4 … a photo on the table.
5 … a t-shirt on the floor.
6 … a lamp on the table.
7 … some posters on the wall.

15 Ask and answer questions about your town.

Is there a river?   *Yes, there is.*
Are there any cinemas?   *No, there aren't.*

1 … an airport?   …
2 … a swimming pool?   …
3 … any internet cafés?   …
4 … any hospitals?   …
5 … a good football team?   …
6 … a sports centre?   …
7 … any English restaurants? …
8 … a chemist?   …

Articles

16 Use *a* or *an* with the words.

1 … apple	5 … idea	9 … class
2 … house	6 … bunk bed	10 … uncle
3 … orange	7 … subject	
4 … course	8 … egg	

17 Complete the sentences with *a*, *an* or *the*.

1 You can use … computer in my bedroom.
2 Vanessa is in … bathroom.
3 I eat … apple for breakfast.
4 Have you done … history homework?
5 We want to buy … new car.
6 They eat … kilo of pasta for lunch!
7 … science teacher is in the classroom.
8 Their mum is … doctor.
9 He's got … poster of … elephant on his bedroom wall.
10 I go to … sports centre at my school on Wednesdays.

GRAMMAR REFERENCE PAGE 98
WORKBOOK PAGE 5

14 Look at the picture. Complete the sentences with *there isn't* and *there aren't*.

1 … any CDs on the table.
2 … a t-shirt on the bed.
3 … a photo on the shelf.
4 … any football posters on the wall.
5 … a computer in the room.
6 … a magazine on the bed.

In the classroom

1 **Match the words in the box with the objects 1–13 in the picture.**

board   chair   student   teacher   wall   cupboard   shelves   bin
dictionary   pencil case   CD player   poster   clock

2 **Complete the questions and the sentences with the verbs in the box.**

speak   mean   spell   copy   read
look up   repeat   say   hand in   open

1   Please … your books at page 8.
2   Can you … the text aloud?
3   How do you … *computer* in your language?
4   What does *rubber* … ?
5   Can you … the question, please?
6   Please … the homework on Wednesday.
7   Can you … up, please? I can't hear you.
8   … the words on the board into your exercise books, please.
9   How do you … *magazine*?
10   Please … the word in your dictionaries.

3 **Who says the sentences in exercise 2? Complete the table.**

Teacher	Teacher or students

Reading

1. **Look at the photos and answer the questions.**

   What can you see in the photos?

   Where do you think the boy is?

2.  **Read the text and check your answers.**

Rob's special friend

1. Mark and I are thirteen years old, and we are very sporty. We often go to the gym – at least three times a week. Mark does exercises to make his arms strong. He can't walk because of a car accident, so he goes everywhere in a wheelchair. But it doesn't stop him doing the things that boys our age want to do.

2. Why do I admire Mark so much? Well, he sometimes feels frustrated and becomes moody, but he never gives up. I play basketball with him and our friends and he always wants to win. Mark's also hard-working at school. People sometimes think he's unfriendly when they first meet him, but he's shy with new people. He always has time for his friends and he tries to help them.

3. If I have a problem, the first person I speak to is Mark. He's very sympathetic and he doesn't ask a lot of questions. He is good at listening. I think that a person that listens to other people is very generous. I don't know a lot of people that are happy to give their time. I'm sometimes selfish so Mark is a good example for me.

4. Mark loves sport, computer games, going on the internet and telling bad jokes. He's just another boy, but he's also different. He's very honest and he's also good fun to be with. That makes him my very special friend.

3 What does Rob think is special about Mark?

4 Complete the sentences with *Mark* or *Rob*.

1 … admires a friend.
2 … wants to win, but he helps his friends.
3 … speaks to a friend if he has a problem.
4 … tells bad jokes but he is good fun.

5 Match the paragraphs 1–4 with a–d. Which paragraph …

a gives examples of how Mark helps Rob?
b is about Mark's favourite pastimes?
c introduces Mark and gives information about his life?
d is about Mark's personality?

6 Answer the questions.

1 Where do Rob and Mark often go?
2 Who does Rob play basketball with?
3 What does Mark always have for his friends?
4 What is Mark good at?
5 What does Mark love?

7 Are the sentences true or false? Explain your answers.

1 Mark does exercises on one part of his body.
2 Mark is a bad student.
3 People always like Mark when they first meet him.
4 Mark doesn't speak a lot when a friend has a problem.
5 Mark's hobbies are different from other people's hobbies.

Vocabulary Personality adjectives

8 Match the definitions 1–10 with the adjectives a–j.

When a person …

1 likes sport a lot,
2 is nervous with people he / she doesn't know,
3 always welcomes new people and is nice to them,
4 often changes from happy to unhappy quickly,
5 tells jokes and makes other people have a good time,
6 only thinks about himself / herself,
7 works twelve hours a day,
8 understands people's problems and helps them,
9 gives people his / her time or money,
10 tells the truth,

we say that he / she is …

a friendly.   f selfish.
b hard-working.   g moody.
c honest.   h shy.
d fun.   i sporty.
e sympathetic.   j generous.

9 Which two adjectives always have a negative meaning?

10 Which three adjectives are made negative with the prefix *un-* (e.g. *happy* / *unhappy*)?

11 *Generous* is the opposite of *selfish*. In the text, find the opposites of these adjectives.

1 sociable   2 lazy

 WORKBOOK PAGES 7, 10

TALK ABOUT IT

1 What qualities do you think make a good friend?

2 Do a survey to find out what the class thinks.

Use adjectives (*friendly*, *sympathetic*, etc.) or expressions (*he / she's good at*, *he / she always has time for …*, etc.) to answer your friends' questions.

Grammar

Present simple

1 **What is special about the two boys in picture 1? What are the pastimes in pictures 2–3?**

2 💿 **Read the text and check your answers.**

David's best friend

My best friend is my twin brother, Michael. We go to Ridgeway school in Manchester, but we don't study in the same class. I like computer studies and maths, but Michael doesn't like science subjects. What does he like? History and languages. We don't like the same subjects, except for PE. We both love sport.

After school, we always play football with our friends. Then we have dinner at eight o'clock and after dinner we do our homework. What do we do at home? Well, I usually go on the internet, but Michael never uses computers. He's usually in his bedroom. He often reads or he listens to music. We're twins and we're best friends, but we sometimes do different things!

3 **Look at the rule and the example sentence.**

> **We use an _s_ at the end of verbs in the 3rd person singular of the present simple.**
> _He often read**s** or he listen**s** to music._

4 **Complete the sentences in the present simple.**

> ask   do   read   play   work

1 My brother always … football after school.
2 My dad … in an office.
3 Karen … her homework in the lunch break.
4 Our friend … the teacher lots of questions.
5 My mum … the newspaper at breakfast.

> **Quick tip** Irregular verbs like _be_ and _have_ have special forms for the 3rd person singular:
> He _is_ good at listening.
> He always _has_ time for his friends.

5 **Complete the sentences with the 3rd person singular form of _be_ or _have_.**

1 My dad … dinner at 10 p.m.
2 My sister … good at basketball.
3 Our teacher always … time for her students.
4 My mum … very friendly with new people.

6 **Look at the rule and the sentences.**

> **We use _don't / doesn't_ + infinitive to make negative sentences in the present simple.**
> _We don't study in the same class._
> _Michael doesn't like science subjects._

7 **Correct the mistakes about Michael and David.**

> They go to school in Liverpool.
> _They don't go to school in Liverpool. They go to school in Manchester._

1 Michael likes computer studies.
2 They play basketball after school.
3 The twins have dinner at six o'clock.
4 David listens to music.

8 **Look at the rule and the example sentences.**

> **We use _do / does_ + subject + infinitive to make present simple questions.**
> _What do we do at home?_
> _What does he like?_

9 **Write questions for the answers.**

1 Sally / play / basketball?
   Yes, she does. She often plays basketball.
2 What / the twins / play after school?
   The twins play football.
3 the twins / go / to the same school?
   Yes, they do. They go to Ridgeway school.
4 When / they / have dinner?
   They have dinner at 8 o'clock.
5 the twins / like / the same subjects?
   No, they don't, except for PE.

Adverbs of frequency

10 *Always* and *never* are adverbs of frequency. Complete the scale with three more examples of adverbs of frequency from exercise 2.

100%	*We always play football with our friends.*
90%	_____
75%	_____
50%	_____
0%	*Michael never uses computers.*

11 Read the rules and the example sentence.

> We put adverbs of frequency after the verb *to be*.
> *I'm sometimes selfish. He's usually in his bedroom.*
>
> We put adverbs of frequency before other verbs:
> *We often go to the gym. He always wants to win.*

Consolidation

12 Complete the dialogue with the words in the box. Then listen and check.

does   like   want   don't   play   doesn't   never
do   know   always   never   does   are   do   is

Beth	Where (1) … you play volleyball, Nina?
Nina	I (2) … play at the gym with my friends.
Beth	(3) … Maria play with you?
Nina	No, she (4) … plays volleyball. She likes basketball. Do you (5) … to play?
Beth	I (6) … know. I'm not very good at volleyball, but I want to do a sport.
Nina	Well, there (7) … some other sports at the gym. (8) … you like gymnastics?
Beth	I (9) … the gymnastics we do at school.
Nina	Great, the gymnastics teacher at the gym (10) … our teacher from school, Mrs Taylor!
Beth	Fantastic! When (11) … she do the classes?
Nina	I don't (12) … . She (13) … do them on Thursdays because we (14) … volleyball then, and she is (15) … at the gym then.
Beth	I can ask her this afternoon.

Object pronouns

13 Complete the text with the object pronouns in the box. Then listen and check.

them   you   her   us   it   me   him   us

When some people meet (1) … they think I'm my twin brother, David. They don't know the difference. Our school friends know; they say I'm more intelligent than (2) … ! In reality, it's easy for (3) … because we study in different classes. When our mother looks at (4) … she always sees the difference. We can't play jokes on (5) … ! When people visit our house they also know the difference. David always uses the computer and he plays on (6) … all the time! What do you think? Look at the picture of (7) … on page 12. Is the difference clear to (8) …?

Question words

14 Complete the questions with the question words in the box. Then answer them with information from the other exercises.

When   How often   Which   What   Who   ~~Where~~

Where does Nina play volleyball?
She plays volleyball at the gym.

1   … does Rob speak to when he has a problem?
2   … subject do Michael and David both like?
3   … do Michael and David do at home?
4   … do Mark and Rob go to the gym?
5   … do the twins do their homework?

GRAMMAR REFERENCE PAGE 100
WORKBOOK PAGE 8

Communication

Vocabulary Pastimes

1 Use words from each box to write the activities in the photos 1–10.

> have   go   play   play   ~~eat~~
> go on   listen to   meet   do
> send

> computer games   gymnastics
> music   the internet   friends
> a picnic   ~~a snack~~
> a text message   volleyball
> shopping

1   *eat a snack*

Listening A summer course

CELTIC SUMMERS

ENGLISH LANGUAGE SUMMER COURSES
GALWAY, IRELAND

Celtic Summers offers children from all over the world the opportunity to learn English in a friendly, cooperative atmosphere.

Sports facilities and lots of activities

From June until September

2 Listen to four friends on an English language summer course. Which of the pastimes in exercise 1 do they talk about?

3 Listen again and decide if the sentences are true or false. Explain your answers.

1   They go to school on Saturdays in Japan.
2   The boys say shopping is interesting.
3   Giovanni meets his friends in an internet café.
4   Lucrecia does sport with her friends.
5   Giovanni says pizza is bad for you.

Speaking At the weekend

4 In pairs, read the dialogue.

> **A** What do you do on Friday evenings?
> **B** I always do my homework.
> **A** Really? I usually play computer games. I always do my homework on Sundays.
> **B** What do you do on Saturdays?
> **A** I usually go swimming with my mum and dad. What do you do?

5 Make up a dialogue about what you do at the weekend. Act out your dialogue in class.

Quick tip   Don't forget to use adverbs of frequency in your dialogue!

WORKBOOK PAGE 10

1  **Read the text.**

Fictional Friends

The important characters in Britain's most popular children's books are children. There are adults, but they are not the stars. There are good adults and bad adults, but it is the young heroes that stop the bad ones. They never need the good adults to help them. They need their friends.

The *Famous Five* stories are a good example. They are now 60 years old but children continue to read them. Why do today's children like them? Well, the *Famous Five* work together and help each other. They don't have computers, the internet or mobile phones. They use human qualities like intelligence and friendship to find solutions to their problems.

Young people obviously like stories about adventure, but they know that friends are very important. We don't have the same adventures that the *Famous Five* have, but in books and in real life friends can help and we can help our friends.

2 **Answer the questions.**

1 Who do the young people in Britain's most popular books need?
2 How old are the *Famous Five* stories?
3 How do the *Famous Five* solve their problems?
4 What type of stories are obviously popular with young people?
5 What do young people know about friends?

TALK ABOUT IT

1 Do you often read?
2 What type of books do you read?
3 Do you read stories in English?

Writing

Description of a friend
Punctuation

1 Match the punctuation symbols 1–5 with their names a–e.

1	,	a	full stop
2	'	b	comma
3	A B C	c	question mark
4	?	d	apostrophe
5	.	e	capital letters

2 Correct the punctuation mistakes in the text.

3 Look at the photos. Which friend is the boy describing?

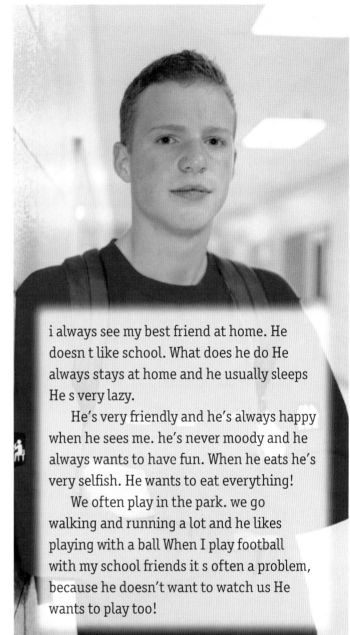

i always see my best friend at home. He doesn t like school. What does he do He always stays at home and he usually sleeps He s very lazy.

He's very friendly and he's always happy when he sees me. he's never moody and he always wants to have fun. When he eats he's very selfish. He wants to eat everything!

We often play in the park. we go walking and running a lot and he likes playing with a ball When I play football with my school friends it s often a problem, because he doesn't want to watch us He wants to play too!

4 Write a description of a friend. Remember to include:

- who he / she is.
- what he / she is like, using adjectives.
- what he / she likes doing and his / her interests.

> **Quick tip** Read your composition carefully and check that the punctuation is correct. Remember to:
> - use capital letters to begin sentences.
> - use apostrophes with *don't*, *doesn't* etc.
> - use commas in long sentences.

 WORKBOOK PAGE 11

Quick check

Vocabulary

1 Choose the correct answer.

1 If you have a problem you can speak to her. She's very **shy / sympathetic**.
2 Fiona is very **generous / honest**. She often gives me her chocolate bar!
3 Mike is **selfish / moody**. He changes from happy to unhappy very quickly.
4 He never does his homework. He isn't very **hard-working / friendly**.
5 They play football, basketball and volleyball every week. They're really **sympathetic / sporty**.

2 Complete the text with the words in the box.

snack   have   a text message   go   go on   do
listen to   basketball   computer games   meet

On Saturdays I do a lot of things. In the morning I (1) … my friends and we (2) … gymnastics at the gym. My brother comes too, but he plays (3) … with his friends. Then we sometimes eat a (4) … at the gym café. In the afternoon we (5) … shopping. Well, we don't buy, but we look! I really like it! At home I sometimes play (6) … or I (7) … the internet. After I (8) … dinner with my family, I go to my room and I (9) … music or send (10) … to my friend.

Vocabulary review

3 Complete the sentences with the words in the box.

science   main course   in front of   at   shelves
dinner

1 The … is the second course in a restaurant.
2 … is the last meal of the day.
3 The … in my bedroom are full of books and magazines.
4 I have maths … 8.30 a.m.
5 My desk is … my bedroom window.
6 My favourite subject is ….

Grammar

4 Put the words in the correct order.

1 usually / they / Do / the gym? / go to
2 They / homework / like / don't.
3 the cinema / go to / We / never.
4 on Saturdays? / go / Where / usually / do / they
5 the classroom / often / in / He's.
6 doesn't / hamburgers / eat / She.
7 always / does / What / she / for breakfast? / have
8 coffee / drinks / Mark / sometimes.

5 Complete the text with the correct object pronouns.

At the weekends I do things with my mum, dad and brother. I usually have a good time with (1) … . Well, my brother is only six and what is interesting for (2) … isn't always interesting for (3) … ! I really like going shopping with my mum. I tell (4) … what I think about the clothes she likes. On Sundays our grandmother usually visits (5) … She has lunch with (6) … , and she really likes (7) … . On Sunday evenings I do my homework. I always have a lot to do. Do your teachers give (8) … a lot of homework? It's not a good way to finish the weekend!

6 Write questions for the answers. Use the words in brackets.

1 We play football after school. (When)
2 Mark is my best friend. (Who)
3 I live in London. (Where)
4 I meet my friends twice a week. (How often)
5 I eat sandwiches for lunch. (What)

Grammar review

7 Correct the mistake in each sentence.

1 She have got two cats.
2 He eat a banana every day.
3 That isn't my pen. It's your.
4 Katies bag is on the desk.
5 Do you want a ice cream?

Reading

1 **Look at the photos and discuss the questions.**

1 Which are your favourite subjects at school?
2 Do you do extra-curricular classes after school or at lunch time? What do you do?

2 **Read the text.**

I WANT TO BE AN ACTRESS

1 Sara Bagur is only thirteen, but she doesn't live at home. Sara wants to be an actress and she is in London. Sara's parents live 400 kilometres away, but they aren't worried about her. In fact they are very happy, because she is studying at the National School for Dramatic Arts, the best theatre school in Britain.
A ….

2 Being at the NSDA is like studying at two schools. B …. She does typical school subjects like maths, science, computer studies and history, and she also does theatre studies classes. Sara can sing and act in plays, and this term the students are preparing a musical. They are rehearsing almost every evening. While Sara is working hard, her friends at normal schools are going out and having fun.

3 However, the NSDA is not always hard work. The students go to the London theatres to study the best actors. They can talk to the actors after the performances. C …. The actors give the students good advice. Sara learns a lot at the school, but she learns even more from speaking to the actors!

4 But Sara and her school friends also work hard at normal subjects. This week Sara isn't acting, she's doing school exams. D …. Only 25% of students at the NSDA find acting jobs when they leave, so the other 75% must be prepared for the real world. Will Sara be one of the lucky 25%? Look out for her name in the future!

3 Match the paragraphs 1–4 with the sentences a–d. Which paragraph is about …

a why it's important to work hard at typical school subjects?
b something the students like doing?
c where Sara lives and studies?
d what subjects Sara studies at the NSDA?

4 Read the text again. Match the sentences 1–4 with the spaces in the text A–D.

1 The students really like doing this.
2 These exams are very important for the students.
3 Sara's parents know she is safe, because she lives at the school too.
4 Sara has a lot more work to do than students at a normal school.

5 Are the sentences true or false? Explain your answers.

1 Sara's parents are worried about her.
2 The NSDA has two schools.
3 She goes out with her friends at normal schools.
4 Sarah learns a lot from the professional actors.
5 75% of the school's students find acting jobs.

6 Answer the questions.

1 Where is Sara studying?
2 Who is rehearsing a musical this term?
3 What does Sara want to be?
4 What do the actors give the students?
5 When is Sara doing school exams?

Vocabulary The arts

7 Match the words in the box with the numbers 1–4.

stage   actor   audience   curtains

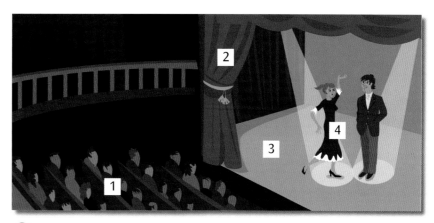

8 Find words in the text to match the definitions 1–8.

1 A theatre production that tells a story.
2 A theatre or cinema production with songs and music.
3 What actors do in theatre or cinema productions.
4 Practising for a theatre production.
5 To make music with your voice.
6 Actors give this every night in a theatre.
7 A very famous actor or singer.

9 Complete the text with the words in the box.

actor   acts   musicals   plays
rehearsing   sings

My favourite (1) … is Ewan McGregor.
He (2) … in films, and in (3) … in the theatre.
He (4) … songs very well. He sometimes uses his talent for music in (5) … . Now he is preparing and (6) … a new film in Hollywood.

 WORKBOOK PAGES 13, 16

TALK ABOUT IT

1 Do you like to watch plays?
Do you perform in plays?

2 Who is your favourite actor / actress? Tell your partner about him / her.

Grammar

Present continuous

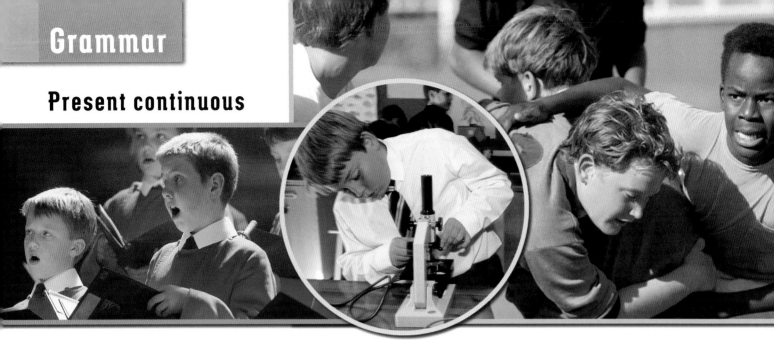

1 🔘 **Listen. Who is singing: boys or girls?**

2 🔘 **What is happening in the photos? Read the text and check your answers.**

An interview with London Music Academy student, Tim Barton.
Who goes to London Music Academy?
Boys aged 8 to 13 that are good at singing.
What do you do at the school?
Obviously we study music, but we also study normal school subjects. We've got a fantastic computer room and this week we're making a choir web page. We also do lots of sports and I usually play rugby, but we aren't playing today. We're jogging and I hate jogging!
What other things are you doing at the moment?
We're recording a CD and we're also rehearsing concerts for our European tour.
Do you prefer singing or playing an instrument?
I love singing in the choir, but I dislike studying music. It's hard work!

3 **Look at the rule. Then match the sentences 1–3 with the forms a–c.**

> **We form the present continuous with the verb *be* + *ing* form.**

1 We aren't playing today.
2 What other things are you doing?
3 We're recording a CD.

a present continuous affirmative
b present continuous negative
c present continuous interrogative

4 **Complete the sentences in the present continuous. Use the verbs in brackets.**

He … an ice cream. (eat)
He's eating an ice cream.

1 They … basketball. (play)
2 She … a song. (sing)
3 I … a text message. (send)
4 You … a DVD. (watch)
5 We … for an exam. (study)
6 He … a t-shirt. (buy)

5 **Write the negative form of the sentences in exercise 4.**

He isn't eating an ice cream.

6 **Write questions in the present continuous.**

they / What / are / buying?
What are they buying?

1 he / Is / today? / working
2 a text message? / she / sending / Is
3 eating? / What / you / are
4 he / writing / Is / a letter?
5 Are / computer games? / playing / you
6 in town? / they / Are / shopping

Present simple or present continuous?

7 Look at the sentences 1–5. Which of them are about …

a activities Tim Barton usually does?
b activities Tim Barton is doing now?

1 We study music and we also study normal school subjects.
2 We're making a web page.
3 We also do lots of sports and I usually play rugby.
4 We aren't playing today. We're jogging.
5 We're recording a CD and we're also rehearsing concerts for our European tour.

8 Complete the rules. Choose the correct answer.

a activities that are happening now.
b activities that have already happened.
c activities that usually happen.

> We use the present simple to talk about … .
> We use the present continuous to talk about … .

9 Complete the sentences about Sara and Tim.

1 I usually … (finish) school at 5 o'clock, but today I … (finish) at lunchtime.
2 Now we … (not rehearse) the musical. We … (talk) to our favourite actors!
3 A What play … you … (study) at the moment?
    B Hamlet. We always … (study) Shakespeare's plays on Mondays.
4 On Saturdays we usually … (do) concerts, but today we … (go) to Paris!
5 A … you … (travel) by plane to Paris?
    B No, we … (travel) by train.

like / hate etc. + *-ing*

10 Look at the sentences and complete the rule.

I hate jogg*ing*.
I love sing*ing* in the choir.

> We use the verbs
> *hate, dislike, don't mind, like, love* + … .

11 Write sentences with the verbs in exercise 10 about these activities.

> act   jog   read in English   go shopping   sing
> do homework   play sport   go out with friends

I don't mind reading in English.

Consolidation

12 Complete the dialogue with the correct present continuous and present simple forms of the verbs in brackets. Then listen and check.

Tim	Mum, we're in Paris and we … (1 walk) to the Eiffel Tower! I really … (2 like) walking here. Paris … (3 have) lots of famous places to see and we … (4 take) lots of photos.
Mum	Yes, it is beautiful. Who … you … (5 visit) the Eiffel Tower with?
Tim	With the teachers except for Mr Dawson. He … (6 hate) visiting places with lots of tourists.
Mum	And … (7 be) the weather good?
Tim	Well, it … (8 not rain) but it's cold.
Mum	Oh Tim, you never … (9 wear) your coat! … you … (10 wear) it now?
Tim	No, Mum. Sorry ! Er, what … you and Dad … (11 do)?
Mum	Well, we … (12 watch) an opera on TV. Your dad … (13 not mind) watching it if he can watch the football later!
Tim	Dad … (14 love) watching football! Well, we … (15 arrive) now, Mum. I'll phone later. Bye! Love to Dad.
Mum	OK, Tim. Have a good time! Bye!

  GRAMMAR REFERENCE PAGE 102
WORKBOOK PAGE 14

Communication

Vocabulary Clothes

1 Match the words in the box with the pictures 1–13.

earrings   dress   trainers   jeans   necklace
jacket   tracksuit   suit   skirt   shirt
trousers   t-shirt   tie

2 What do you think? Are there any clothes in exercise 1 that are only for boys or only for girls?

Listening The party

3 What are the people wearing in the picture?

4 Listen. Choose the correct answer.

1 When Andy speaks to his mum he's wearing …
 a a tracksuit   b shirt and trousers.
2 Andy's shirt is a present from his …
 a sister   b grandmother.
3 Diane is putting on her …
 a jeans   b necklace.
4 Her mum … the clothes Diane's wearing.
 a likes   b doesn't like.
5 His mum tells Andy to …
 a find their father.   b get changed.

Speaking What are you wearing?

5 In pairs, read the dialogue.

A What are you wearing now?
B I'm wearing jeans, trainers and a t-shirt.
A And what do you like wearing at home?
B I like wearing a tracksuit.
A And what do you wear when you go to school?

6 Make up a dialogue about what you are wearing. Act out your dialogue in class.

➡ WORKBOOK PAGE 16

Culture focus

1 Match the photos 1–3 with the performers a–c.

a   a juggler   b   a contortionist   c   acrobats

2 Match the numbers 1–5 on the map with the countries in the box.

> Mongolia   China   Ukraine   Canada   the USA

A day at the circus

The Cirque du Soleil is from Montreal, Canada, but the circus artists are from all over the world. The Cirque has ten different shows, and each show is like a musical, telling an incredible story. Our reporter, Chris Adams, meets some of the young stars at the circus.

Ruslana and Taisiya Bazaliy

Ruslana and Taisiya are identical twins from Ukraine. They are acrobats and school students, too. Ruslana tells us that a typical day is school, the show, and then homework.

Now they are rehearsing and I'm watching them from the stage. It's incredible, the girls are flying above my head!

Enkhjargal Dashbaljir

Enkhjargal is a contortionist from Mongolia, and she does gymnastics and dances. At the moment she's performing in Las Vegas, USA, and she loves working for the Cirque du Soleil. People really like watching her performance. She's so flexible!

Wang Wei Yi

Wang Wei Yi is a twelve year-old juggler from China. Wang and her friends use a piece of string to control a round piece of wood. It sounds easy, but it's impossible!

The girls are now practising some moves to music. They're wearing traditional dresses with long sleeves. It's a beautiful performance.

3 Read the text. Then match the sentences 1–6 with the names in the box.

> Wang Wei Yi   Enkhjargal Dashbaljir
> Ruslana Bazaliy   The Cirque du Soleil

1 She works to music.
2 She talks about what she does every day.
3 She's working in the USA at the moment.
4 It tells 10 stories.
5 She wears clothes from her country.
6 She works with her sister.

TALK ABOUT IT

1 Would you like to work in a circus?

2 In Britain many people think it is a bad thing that circuses have animals like lions, tigers and elephants. Do you agree? Why?

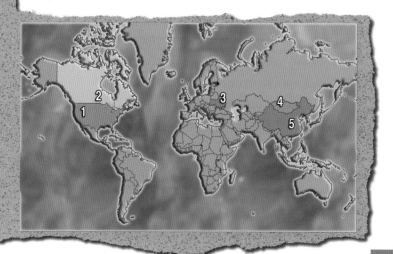

Writing

An email *and and but*

1 **Complete the sentences with *and* and *but*.**

We use … to show one thing or idea is different to another.
We use … to connect words and parts of sentences.

2 **Complete the email with *and* and *but*.**

Dear Patrick,

How are you? This is just a quick email to tell you about what I'm doing. I'm in the computer room at school (**1**) … I'm writing on a computer here. I've got a lot of work because we're rehearsing a school play every night (**2**) … we've also got exams. I love doing the play (**3**) … I don't really like doing exams!
The play we're performing is Hamlet by William Shakespeare (**4**) … I'm Hamlet! I'm very happy to be Hamlet (**5**) … our English teacher is good fun, (**6**) … there are lots of difficult lines to remember. It's hard work! To remember or not remember, that is the question!
Well, I want to write more (**7**) … I've got to study for tomorrow's maths exam. What are you doing at the moment? Have you got exams? Send me an email (**8**) … tell me!
Bye!
Andy

3 **Match the sentence parts 1–8 and a–h with *and* or *but*.**

1 James doesn't like playing basketball
2 Ewan can act
3 I want to go to the cinema
4 We go to the gym
5 Jane is hard-working
6 My mother is shopping
7 We've got a maths exam today
8 It's raining

and
but

a … they're playing tennis.
b … I've got a lot of homework.
c … an English exam tomorrow.
d … he can sing; he's very talented!
e … my father is helping her.
f … we do gymnastics.
g … her brother is very lazy.
h … his sister loves playing it.

4 **Write an email to a friend. Look at Andy's email to help you. Remember to:**

• tell your friend why you are writing.
• use *and* when you tell him / her about what you're doing at the moment.
• use *and* and *but* to talk about what you like and don't like doing.
• ask him / her about what he / she is doing at the moment.
• ask him / her to send you an email soon.
• finish your email.

 WORKBOOK PAGE 17

Quick check

Vocabulary

1 Complete the sentences with the words in the box.

> star   rehearsing   stage   musical   act
> performance   play

1   He's an actor, but he isn't famous. He isn't a … .
2   In a … the actors … and sing.
3   William Shakespeare is the author of a … called *Hamlet*.
4   We're … a new play. We've got five weeks to practise before the first … .
5   When I'm on … in the theatre, I can see lots of faces looking at me.

2 Answer the questions with the words in the box.

> shirt   trousers   earring   tie   dress
> tracksuit   jacket   trainers

1   What do men sometimes wear around their neck?
2   What two things do you wear to play sport?
3   Which two things make a suit?
4   What do men usually wear with a suit?
5   What can a woman wear from her neck to her ankles?
6   Which item of jewellery usually comes in a pair?

Vocabulary review: Units 1–2

3 Choose the correct answer.

I like doing lots of things, but at the weekends I always go (1) **shopping / internet**. I (2) **go / meet** my friends and we go to clothes shops and look at the new (3) **dresses / computer games**. The people in the shop we usually go to are very (4) **friendly / sporty** and helpful. In the evenings I love watching actors on the (5) **performance / stage** in the theatre. My friends prefer new films with famous (6) **stars / rehearsing**, so we do different things every week. But the best thing is being with my friends. They're (7) **selfish / fun** and we always have a great time.

Grammar

4 Write positive or negative sentences and questions in the present continuous. Use the verbs in the box.

> play   wear   sing   ~~study~~   do   travel

Sara / a theatre school **?**
Is Sara studying at a theatre school?

1   They / exams today ✗
2   he / in the choir **?**
3   I / by plane ✔
4   She / a white dress ✔
5   I / computer games ✗

5 Complete the scale with the verbs in the box.

> don't mind   like   hate   ~~love~~   dislike

++   I *love* reading.
+   I … cycling.
+ – I … learning maths.
–   I … shopping.
– – I … doing exams!

6 Complete the sentences with the verbs in the box.

> travel   eat   do   play   study

1   We love … English.
2   I dislike … gymnastics.
3   She doesn't mind … volleyball.
4   They like … pizza.
5   I hate … by boat.

Grammar review: Units 1–2

7 Complete the text with the correct present simple or present continuous forms of the verbs.

James always … (1 go) to theatre rehearsals at school on Tuesdays and today they … (2 rehearse) the school play. He usually … (3 act) in school plays but he … (4 not act) in this play. Now he … (5 play) a guitar in the school orchestra and at the moment they … (6 learn) the songs for the play. He never … (7 sing) because he's not very good at it. They … (8 not want) the audience to go home!

Reading

1 Look at the photos 1–3 and answer the questions.

Can you name the programmes? Which of the programmes do you like?

Do you know what type of programmes these are?

2 Read the text and check your ideas.

Watching all around the world

A lot of young people around the world watch television. But are they watching the same programmes? What do the world's young people think about TV?

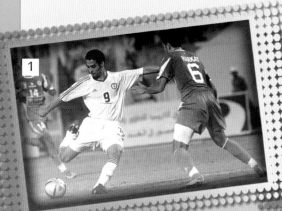

Paula, Canada

I watch television for about three hours a day. Satellite TV has really cool quiz shows and it shows the funniest comedy programmes. Satellite TV is better than cable TV. I also think the internet is fun. I send emails to my friends about our favourite soaps!

Mamadou, Mali

A few years ago television in my country was terrible, but now it's better. We have two channels. The first channel shows news and documentaries. I think the second channel is more interesting - there are sports programmes and old films. I watch sports programmes for about five hours a week, but I prefer playing football with my friends. Who wants to sit at home?

Keiko, Japan

Last year I could watch TV a lot, but now I go to a bigger school, a secondary school, and I have a lot of homework. I also play baseball in the school team. The best programmes for young people are *Manga* cartoons. In fact most *Manga* fans are older than me, because there are *Manga* cartoons for all ages. They're fantastic!

Yolanda, Spain

I probably watch TV for two hours a day. When I get home, I do my homework, then I play computer games or I watch TV. I think soaps are great. I never watch reality shows like *Big Brother* - they're the most boring programmes. We always talk about our favourite TV programmes at school.

3 Who do you think isn't as interested in TV as the other young people? Why?

4 Read the text again. Answer the questions.

Who ...

1   does his / her homework before watching TV?
2   thinks playing football is more fun than watching TV?
3   doesn't have much time to watch TV?
4   talks about TV programmes at school?
5   sends emails about soaps?
6   do you think watches TV the most?

5 Complete the table.

	Hours watching TV	Favourite programmes
Paula		
Mamadou		
Keiko	–	
Yolanda		

6 Which other activites do Paula, Mamadou, Keiko and Yolanda like?

Paula likes the internet…

7 Answer the questions.

1   Why does Paula like satellite TV?
2   Which channel is more interesting in Mali?
3   Which activity does Mamadou like more than watching TV?
4   Why doesn't Keiko often watch TV this year?
5   Which people are older than Keiko?

Vocabulary Programmes

8 Match the types of programmes in the box with programmes in the TV guide.

cartoons   the news   documentary   reality show   quiz show
film   the weather forecast   soap   comedy programme
sports programme   cookery programme

This week's best TV programmes

Heart of the City
Monday, Tuesday, Wednesday and Thursday 7 p.m. BBC 1
Vanessa is having big family problems but she can't tell anybody. She's very unhappy.

Cross and Stripe
Monday 9.45 p.m. ITV 1
Joe Cross and John Stripe with lots of good fun and some terrible jokes!

I'm an Intellectual
Tuesday 7.45 p.m. BBC 1
The contestants have five seconds to answer the questions.

Fantastic Food!
Wednesday 7 p.m. ITV 2
This week we learn how to make delicious chocolate brownies!

Goal!
Wednesday 8.30 p.m. Channel 5
Tonight it's Manchester United against Barcelona.

In the Jungle
Thursday 6 p.m. Channel 4
Great photography of tigers in the Indian jungle.

Pirates of the Caribbean
Friday 10 p.m. BBC 2
An adventure story to finish the week.

Survivors
Friday 10.30 p.m. Channel 5
Ten celebrities living on an island.

Disney Club
Saturday 10 a.m. ITV 2
Our children's favourite programme.

Weekly Report
Saturday 10 p.m. BBC 1
This week's political and economic news.

Local Weather
Saturday 10.30 p.m. BBC1
Sun, rain or snow next week? Find out!

 WORKBOOK PAGES 19, 22

TALK ABOUT IT

1   How many hours of TV do you watch every day?
2   Which TV programmes do you hate?
3   Which TV programmes do you prefer?
4   Which TV personalities do you like / dislike?

Grammar

Comparatives and superlatives

1 🔵 **Read the text and match the bars on the graph a–e with the countries.**

> The biggest TV watchers in the world are American children. They watch TV for four hours a day. Is TV as popular as that in Europe? The British think watching TV is the coolest free time activity, and they watch it for three hours a day. TV is more popular in Spain than in France – the Spanish watch it for two and a half hours a day and the French watch it for two hours. Finally, in Sweden, TV isn't as popular as it is in the other countries – the Swedes only watch it for one hour a day. The Swedes say they are happier than other nationalities because they do cooler activities than watching TV!

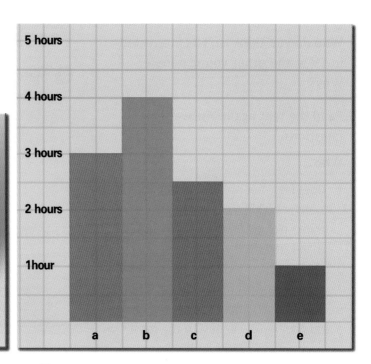

2 **Look at the table. For each type of adjective A–D, find another comparative and a superlative example from the texts on page 26 and this page.**

	Adjective	Comparative	Superlative
A	clean	cleaner	the cleanest
B	thin	thinner	the thinnest
C	friendly	friendlier	the friendliest
D	expensive	more expensive	the most expensive

> **Quick tip** There are also some irregular adjectives. Find out the comparative and superlative forms of *good*, *bad* and *far*.

3 **Write comparative sentences.**

Summer / hot / winter.
Summer is hotter than winter.

1 Reality programmes / interesting / the weather forecast.
2 Spain / sunny / England.
3 I / tall / my mum.
4 The USA / big / Sweden.
5 An MP3 player / expensive / a DVD player.
6 She / nice/ her sister.
7 Gloria / pretty / her cousin.

> **Quick tip** When we write comparative sentences we use *than* not *that*:
> Most *Manga* fans are older *than* me.
> TV is more popular in Spain *than* in France.

4 **Complete the sentences with the superlative form of the adjectives in brackets.**

1 Antarctica is … (cold) place in the world.
2 France is … (popular) country in the world for tourists.
3 The … (sunny) place in the world is in Arizona, USA.
4 Paris is … (expensive) city in Europe.
5 Asia is … (big) continent in the world.
6 The Mojave desert in California, USA is … (hot) place in the world.

5 **Look at the rule and the example sentence.**

> We can make negative comparisons by using *not as* + adjective + *as*.
> In Sweden, TV isn't as popular as it is in the other countries.

6 **Write sentences using *not as … as*.**

Nadia / friendly / Sarah.
Nadia isn't as friendly as Sarah.

1 He / happy / his sister.
2 History / difficult / Maths.
3 Cable TV / good / satellite TV
4 Watching TV / important / doing homework.
5 My sister and my brother / tall / me.
6 Dubai / big / Paris.
7 My mother / old / my father.

can

7 Terry wants to make a film but he hasn't got much money. Complete the interview. Use *can / can't*.

Interviewer	Terry, **(1)** … you make a film with only £1000? Lots of people say it isn't possible!
Terry	Yes, I **(2)** … . It's easy to do! You **(3)** … find cheap actors, and you **(4)** … ask for help from friends. With help you **(5)** … fail!
Interviewer	But **(6)** … you have special effects?
Terry	That's a problem! You **(7)** … make special effects cheaply. They're expensive!

8 What can you do? Ask and answer questions with a partner. Use *can / can't*.

Can you speak French? No, I can't.

> **Quick tip** Be careful with questions! We don't say *do you can…?* We say *Can you…?*

must

9 Read the rules. Which sentence is correct: 1 or 2?

> We use *must* and *mustn't* for obligation and strong advice.
>
> *Must* and *mustn't* are followed by the infinitive, but we don't use *to*.

1 You must finish your dinner.
2 You must to finish your dinner.

10 What must Terry do? Choose the correct answer.

1 He **must / mustn't** choose Hollywood film stars.
2 He **must / mustn't** find an interesting story.
3 He **must / mustn't** look for a good location.
4 He **must / mustn't** use expensive special effects.
5 He **must / mustn't** spend too much money.

11 Write five sentences about school rules. Use *must / mustn't*.

You mustn't arrive late.

Past simple: *be* and *can*

12 Complete the text with *was / wasn't, were / weren't* and *could / couldn't*.

Nasubi, a young Japanese man, **(1)** … in a small room for fifteen months. Why? He **(2)** … the star of a Japanese reality TV programme. There **(3 ✗)** … any contact with his friends, and he **(4 ✗)** … phone his family. But he **(5)** … send postcards and he **(6)** … speak to the people in the TV studio. There **(7 ✗)** … any modern machines like TVs or computers in his room, so he **(8 ✗)** … use the internet but there **(9)** … some books. A boring programme? Well, not for the Japanese. There **(10)** … a big audience every week watching Nasubi!

Consolidation

13 Complete the text. When there is an adjective, use the correct form. For the other spaces, use *was / were* or *could / couldn't*.

Today it's … **(1 easy)** than before to watch films, record music, and communicate with people . But are our lives … **(2 interesting)** than our grandparents' lives? Are we … **(3 happy)** than they were? Our grandparents **(4)** … send emails and they **(5)** … phone their friends on mobile phones, but then there **(6)** … more time for family and friends. They **(7)** … tell stories, and they **(8)**… good at inventing fun activities. Today, we are … as … **(9 not / good)** as our grandparents **(10)** … at communicating. Some people think technology is the … **(11 important)** thing in our lives. It isn't – people are! We have the … **(12 good)** computers, plasma TVs, DVD and MP3 players in our homes, but we don't speak to each other enough!

 GRAMMAR REFERENCE PAGE 103
WORKBOOK PAGE 20

Communication

Vocabulary Strong adjectives

1. Match the strong adjectives in the box with the adjectives 1–6.

> great   hilarious   ~~fantastic~~   astonishing
> terrible   brilliant   horrible   terrifying   awful
> fascinating   wonderful

1 really good *fantastic* … … …
2 extremely funny …
3 very surprising …
4 extremely interesting …
5 very bad … … …
6 really frightening …

2. Replace the adjectives in the advert with strong adjectives.

Teen Magazine

This month's edition of Teen magazine is out now!

Inside there are **extremely interesting** articles about your favourite film and TV stars and there's a **very surprising** interview with actor Will Smith; he tells Teen magazine some exclusive secrets about his life! There's another episode in our **extremely funny** and **really frightening** story "The Nightmare" and there's also a **really good** competition. We want you to write and tell us about your **very bad** holiday experiences!

All this and more in Teen magazine – The best magazine on the market!

Listening Adverts

3. Listen to the radio adverts. What type of products are they talking about?

4. Listen again and answer the questions.

MUNCHIPOPS THEY'RE CHOCO-FANTASTIC!

1 To enter the competition, do you send six *Munchipops* chocolates or six *Munchipops* packets?
2 Which date do they talk about in the *Munchipops* advert: December 31st or December 13th?
3 What are the names of the two footballers in the *All-Star Football* advert?
4 How much is the *All-Star Football* computer game?
5 Who is the shoe shop for?
6 What percentage (%) discount is there for young students?

Speaking TV adverts

5. In pairs, read the dialogue.

> A Which TV advert do you think is best?
> B I like the one for Kiwi Kola because it's hilarious. I like funny TV ads.
> A And what do you think the worst TV advert is?
> B The ad for Jordan's burgers is terrible. The music is awful and the people are worse than the music!

6. Make up a dialogue about what you think about TV adverts. Act out your dialogue in class.

 WORKBOOK PAGE 22

Culture focus

1 **Look at the photos 1–4 and discuss the questions.**

What is happening in the photos?

Divide the photos into two groups. What is the difference between them?

Which of the activities in the photos do you do?

2 🔘 **Read the text. Which photo best matches the text?**

CONTROL YOUR TV!

Some of the most popular TV programmes are about people who do interesting things. Is your life like that or do you watch TV all the time?

Imagine switching on TV and seeing two boys in their bedrooms watching television – possibly the most boring programme on TV! But lots of families spend hours watching other people live fictitious lives. In the USA some people spend ten years of their lives watching television! It isn't very exciting!

Television has other negative effects. Studies in the USA show that today's children are fatter than children were before. When they're watching TV, American children eat and eat! Other studies show that children that watch a lot of TV are worse students than those that watch less.

Of course, television has some good points. We can watch the news and find out what is happening in the world. The TV shows exciting sports events and concerts that we haven't got the time or the money to go to. And watching a film or comedy programme with friends or family is good fun.

So, the message is clear – we have to control what, and how much we watch. The people that do this have healthier lives, are better students and have more fun!

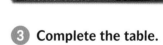

3 **Complete the table.**

Bad things about TV	Good things about TV
1 …	1 …
2 …	2 …
3 …	3 …

TALK ABOUT IT

1 Which activities do you think are the most interesting, the worst etc.?

2 Which activities do you think are fascinating, terrible, etc.?
(Remember to use strong adjectives.)

Writing

1

2

A report Organising information

1 Name the activities in the photos. Which do you do at school and which do you do after school?

2 Look at the information and read the report.

The most popular school activities

Boys
- playing in a school sports team 26%
- acting in a school play 16%
- going on school trips 22%
- eating with friends 17%
- going to class 19%

Girls
- playing in a school sports team 9%
- acting in a school play 15%
- eating with friends 27%
- going on school trips 25%
- going to class 24%

a This report is about the most popular school activities for students. I have answers from all the students in my class, First Year Group A. I also have answers from some students from First Year Group B.

b The coolest school activity for boys is playing in a school sports team, and for girls it's eating with friends. Both boys and girls like school trips and going to class, but these activities are more interesting for the girls than for the boys. Acting in a school play isn't as popular for girls as it is for boys.

c In conclusion, I think this information is fascinating. The most surprising thing is that boys and girls like doing the same activities, and that we are not very different.

3 Match the parts of the report 1–3 with the paragraphs a-c.

1 the conclusion
2 the introduction
3 the important information

4 You are going to write a report about the information below. First, make notes about the most popular free-time activities for young people.

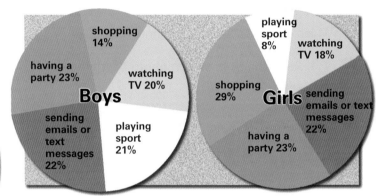

Boys
- shopping 14%
- having a party 23%
- watching TV 20%
- sending emails or text messages 22%
- playing sport 21%

Girls
- playing sport 8%
- watching TV 18%
- shopping 29%
- sending emails or text messages 22%
- having a party 23%

5 Plan your introduction.

- What is the report about?
- Who do you have information from?

6 Plan what you can say about the information.

- What are the most popular activities?
- Compare the most popular activities for boys and girls.

7 Plan your conclusion.

- Is the information interesting?
- What is the most surprising thing?

8 Use your notes to write a report. Use the text from exercise 2 to help you.

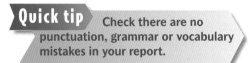

Quick tip Check there are no punctuation, grammar or vocabulary mistakes in your report.

WORKBOOK PAGE 23

Quick check

Vocabulary

1 Which type of TV programme …

1   shows us how to make nice things to eat?
2   tells us what is happening in our country and in the world today?
3   makes us laugh?
4   is usually for children?
5   shows football, basketball and volleyball?
6   gives us a prediction for the weather?

2 Complete the table with adjectives.

Adjectives	Strong adjectives
(1) …	fantastic, great, brilliant, wonderful
(2) …	hilarious
(3) …	astonishing
(4) …	fascinating
(5) …	terrible, horrible, awful
(6) …	terrifying

Vocabulary review: Units 1–3

3 Write the opposites of these adjectives.

1   friendly   3   sympathetic
2   selfish   4   hard-working

4 Which word is not correct in each group?

1   volleyball   gymnastics   football   basketball
2   generous   moody   friendly   sympathetic
3   necklace   jeans   trousers   tights
4   act   sing   dance   stage

5 Match the verbs in the box with the nouns 1–10.

send   listen to   do   go   eat   play   meet
go on   have   play

1 … a snack   6 … the internet
2 … friends   7 … music
3 … lunch   8 … gymnastics
4 … volleyball   9 … a text message
5 … shopping   10 … computer games

Grammar

6 Complete the table.

Adjective	Comparative	Superlative
hot	(1) …	(2) …
(3) …	older	(4) …
(5) …	(6) …	the laziest
important	(7) …	(8) …
(9) …	better	(10) …
bad …	(11) …	(12) …

7 Write sentences using *not as … as*.

My MP3 player / *good* / your MP3 player.
My MP3 player isn't as good as your MP3 player.

1   We / happy / them.
2   Computer games / interesting / the internet.
3   The other channels / popular / cable TV.
4   American TV / good / European TV.
5   Cookery programmes / exciting / sports programmes.
6   A CD / expensive / a DVD.

8 Complete the sentences with *was / wasn't, were / weren't*, or *could / couldn't*.

1   When we … 13 years old, my friend and I … swim. But now we can!
2   40 years ago I … run very fast. I was the best athlete at the school.
3   When I … at school I couldn't do maths. I … good at maths!
4   We … good at basketball at my school. We couldn't win a game!

Grammar review: Units 1–3

9 Correct the mistake in each sentence.

1   I play often football.
2   My brother lives in London. On holidays I visit he.
3   She always drink water at lunch time.
4   Tim loves play football.
5   At the moment I is playing a computer game.
6   She's gooder at history than geography.

Revision: Units 1-3

Vocabulary

1 **Put these words into pairs of opposites.**

~~friendly~~ unsympathetic selfish lazy
~~unfriendly~~ hard-working shy generous
sociable boring unhappy terrible
fascinating sympathetic fantastic happy

Positive	Negative
friendly	*unfriendly*

2 **Make the sentence parts 1–10 with a–j.**

1 My parents are having …
2 I'm meeting …
3 At school we usually eat …
4 I like listening to …
5 I send …
6 My sister plays …
7 We sometimes go on …
8 My mum likes going …
9 We do …
10 I think playing …

a … the internet at school to practise English.
b … shopping on Saturdays.
c … computer games is boring.
d … a special dinner on their 25th anniversary.
e … volleyball in the school team.
f … gymnastics on Tuesdays and Thursdays.
g … my friends at the cinema.
h … a snack at ten o'clock in the morning.
i … music in my bedroom.
j … text messages to my friends when I'm in bed.

3 **Complete the sentences with the words in the box.**

reality shows stage cookery programme act
rehearse sing play the weather forecast

1 A good actor in a musical can … and … .
2 The people in … aren't actors. They're real people.
3 A lot of people watch … after the news.
4 TV actors work in a studio, but theatre actors work on the … .
5 The chef makes delicious food on the … .
6 Before the first performance of a …, the actors …

4 **What are they wearing in the photos 1–3? Choose words from the box.**

t-shirt trainers jacket tracksuit suit shirt
necklace jeans

5 **Choose the correct answers.**

Tom Do you think maths is interesting?
Emma Interesting? It's **(1) astonishing / fascinating**!
Tom Really? I'm very bad at maths. The teacher says my homework is always **(2) awful / terrifying**. And we've got an exam next week. Maths exams are **(3) terrifying / wonderful**!
Emma No, biology exams are the frightening exams for me.
Tom Oh no, biology is really **(4) cool / surprising**. Mrs Davenport's lessons are great, and she always tells good jokes. She's **(5) hilarious / unfriendly**.
Emma Well, yes she's very **(6) bad / funny**, but biology isn't! Look, I've got a good idea; I can help you with maths and you can help me with biology. What do you think?
Tom That's a **(7) great / horrible** idea!

Grammar

1 Write sentences about Barbara and you. Use adverbs of frequency.

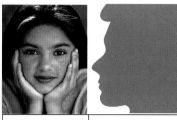

	Barbara	Me
(1) be shy	never	*sometimes*
(2) go shopping	often	
(3) eat snacks	always	
(4) do gymnastics	usually	
(5) be lazy	sometimes	

1 *Barbara is never shy.*
I'm sometimes shy.

2 Complete the sentences with object pronouns.

1 I'm good at languages, but science and maths are difficult for ... .
2 My brother isn't very good at tennis – I always beat ... .
3 I'm looking for my sister. I can't find ... !
4 I've got a new computer game. I love playing ... .
5 We live in London. Come and visit ... !
6 My cousins go to the same school as me. I see ... every day.
7 You got 100% in the French exam. French is easy for ... !

3 Complete the questions for the answers in brackets. Use the words in the box.

How often   When   Who   Where   Which   What

1 ... do you meet at the cinema? (My friend.)
2 ... do you do at the weekend? (Meet friends.)
3 ... does she play basketball? (Twice a week.)
4 ... does the gymnastics class start? (At 4.30 pm.)
5 ... do you do your homework? (In my bedroom.)
6 ... school do you go to? (Silver Street school.)

4 Write affirmative and negative sentences and questions in the present simple.

1 David Beckham / play football ✓
2 We / live in London ✗
3 Your dad / work for the United Nations ?
4 My mum / eat cereal for breakfast ✓
5 I / go to bed at five o'clock ✗
6 They / learn English ?

5 Complete the text. Use the present continuous form of the verbs in the box.

study   eat   read   listen
rehearse   play   drink   play

"...well it's break time now, mum, and it's raining. We're all in the classroom. Dave (1) ... pizza, Dale (2) ... fruit juice and Julia and Mary (3) ... to music. Jimmy and Kevin (4) ... football, Phil (5) ... his guitar and Anna, Darren and Vanessa (6) ... the school play. Studying? Well, Clare and Frank (7) ... maths, and Adam (8) ... a book in French. Oh, I must go! The teacher is coming!"

6 Write sentences in the present continuous negative form.

Phil / eat / pizza.
Phil isn't eating pizza.
1 Anna, Darren and Vanessa / play / football.
2 Julia and Mary / study / maths.
3 Dave / drink / fruit juice.
4 Clare and Frank / sing.
5 Adam / play / the guitar.

7 **Write questions in the present continuous..**

1 … ? (they / in the library)
No, they aren't. They're studying in a classroom.
2 … ? (your sister / a play)
No, she isn't. She's rehearsing a musical.
3 … ? (your friends / volleyball).
No, they aren't. They're playing basketball.
4 … ? (you / a magazine).
No, I'm not. I'm reading a book in English.

8 **Complete the sentences with the verbs in brackets. Use the present simple or the present continuous.**

1 At the moment I … a letter, but I usually … emails. (write)
2 Today my best friend … a dress, but she often … jeans. (wear)
3 Tim Barton usually … in a choir, but this afternoon he … in a rock group. (sing)
4 I usually … cereals for breakfast, but this morning I … toast and marmalade. (eat)
5 We always … the internet at school, but today we … the internet at the internet café. (go on)
6 This evening she … a travel programme, but she often … chat shows. (watch)

9 **Write sentences using the verbs in the box.**

don't mind   like   hate   love   dislike

1 My best friend / ++ / do / gymnastics.
2 I / – / wear / a shirt and suit.
3 My parents / – – / travel / by plane.
4 My friends / +/– / study / for exams.
5 We / + / act / in the school play.

10 **Write comparative sentences.**

1 Clare / tall / Sue.
2 Snowboarding / exciting / skiing.
3 London / big / Paris.
4 History / interesting / geography.
5 David / happy / Nick.

11 **Complete the sentences with the superlative form of the adjectives in brackets.**

1 She is … (nice) girl in the school.
2 Paul is … (young) student in my class.
3 You are … (lazy) person I know!
4 Manchester United is … (famous) English team.
5 Today is the … (hot) day of the year.

12 **Write the sentences again with *not as … as*.**

Paris is bigger than Athens.
Athens isn't as big as Paris.

1 English is easier than German.
2 Cartoons are better than films.
3 My sister is lazier than my brother.
4 Soaps are more interesting than the news.
5 American food is worse than English food.

13 **Choose the correct answer.**

1 You **can** / **can't** visit the moon today.
2 You **can** / **can't** play tennis without a racket.
3 You **can** / **can't** act in the school play if you rehearse.
4 You **must** / **mustn't** be nice to your friends.
5 You **must** / **mustn't** study for the exams.
6 You **must** / **mustn't** forget your mum's birthday.

14 **Complete the dialogue with *was / wasn't, were / weren't* and *could / couldn't*.**

John	Granddad, was life different when you (1) … young?
Granddad	Oh yes! We (2) … email people because there (3) …any computers! But we (4) …play in the streets. There (5) …a lot of cars then and it (6) …dangerous.
John	What about holidays?
Granddad	We (7) …go by plane then because it (8) … very expensive. My best holiday (9) … in France. There (10) … some friendly French children. We are still good friends today! You can't make friends like that on a computer!

Consolidation

1 Look at the answers below. Choose the correct answer for each space.

My parents always (1) … that TV is bad for you, but I think there (2) … some great programmes on TV. And the (3) … thing about television is when you go to school the next day and you talk about your favourite programmes with your friends. At the moment (4) … all watching a (5) … from Australia. There are lots of young (6) … in it and they have the same problems and experiences as (7) … . It's really cool! Of course we know that there are (8) … interesting things to do, but TV isn't as (9) … as adults say. Another good thing is that TV is free. The circus

(10) … in my city today and I want to go, but the tickets are very (11) … . I can't go! When I have some money I go to the cinema. I (12) … on Friday evenings with my friends. We (13) … at 6 pm and then we eat a (14) … before the film. We don't mind (15) … musicals, comedies, or detective stories; we just (16) … starting the weekend at the cinema and films are always better at the cinema (17) … on TV. I usually arrive home at 9 p.m., and I always find my parents and (18) … brother in the sitting room, watching television of course!

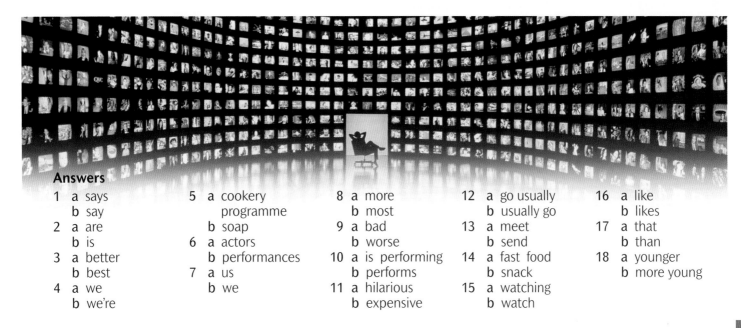

Answers

1	a says	5	a cookery	8	a more	12	a go usually	16	a like
	b say		programme		b most		b usually go		b likes
2	a are		b soap	9	a bad	13	a meet	17	a that
	b is	6	a actors		b worse		b send		b than
3	a better		b performances	10	a is performing	14	a fast food	18	a younger
	b best	7	a us		b performs		b snack		b more young
4	a we		b we	11	a hilarious	15	a watching		
	b we're				b expensive		b watch		

Reading

1 Look at the picture and answer the questions.

Do you think the text is a newspaper article, a story or an interview? What do you think it is about?

2 Read the first paragraph. What do you think happened in Chapter One?

Chapter Two

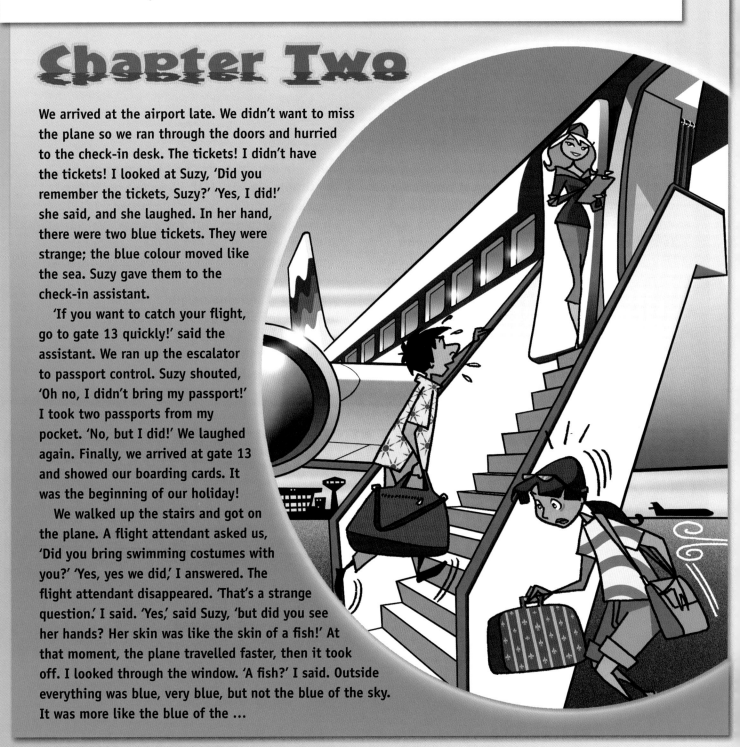

We arrived at the airport late. We didn't want to miss the plane so we ran through the doors and hurried to the check-in desk. The tickets! I didn't have the tickets! I looked at Suzy, 'Did you remember the tickets, Suzy?' 'Yes, I did!' she said, and she laughed. In her hand, there were two blue tickets. They were strange; the blue colour moved like the sea. Suzy gave them to the check-in assistant.

'If you want to catch your flight, go to gate 13 quickly!' said the assistant. We ran up the escalator to passport control. Suzy shouted, 'Oh no, I didn't bring my passport!' I took two passports from my pocket. 'No, but I did!' We laughed again. Finally, we arrived at gate 13 and showed our boarding cards. It was the beginning of our holiday!

We walked up the stairs and got on the plane. A flight attendant asked us, 'Did you bring swimming costumes with you?' 'Yes, yes we did,' I answered. The flight attendant disappeared. 'That's a strange question.' I said. 'Yes,' said Suzy, 'but did you see her hands? Her skin was like the skin of a fish!' At that moment, the plane travelled faster, then it took off. I looked through the window. 'A fish?' I said. Outside everything was blue, very blue, but not the blue of the sky. It was more like the blue of the ...

3 🔘 Read the the rest of the text. What unusual things did Dave and Suzy notice at the airport and on the plane?

4 Read the story again and order the events 1–6.

a The flight attendant asked Dave and Suzy a question.
b Dave took the passports from his pocket.
c Dave and Suzy talked about the flight attendant's hands.
d Dave and Suzy showed their boarding cards.
e Dave and Suzy ran up the escalator.
f The check-in assistant told Dave and Suzy to go to gate 13.

5 Which two things happened after Dave and Suzy talked about the flight attendant's hands?

6 Answer the questions with the names in the box.

Dave   the flight attendant
Suzy   the check-in assistant
Dave and Suzy

Who …

1 didn't have the tickets?
2 didn't bring a passport?
3 told Dave and Suzy to hurry?
4 ran in the airport?
5 disappeared?

7 Choose the correct answer.

1 Suzy and Dave wanted to …
   a miss the plane. b go on holiday.
2 Suzy and Dave ran up the escalator to …
   a the plane.   b passport control.
3 Suzy shouted about her passport at …
   a gate 13.   b passport control.

Vocabulary Travel

8 Match the words in the box with the definitions 1–6.

gate   boarding card   passport   catch   ticket
flight attendant   miss   escalator

1 A person that works on a plane.
2 A verb that means *take* a plane, bus or train.
3 Three documents you need to travel on a plane.
4 Moving stairs that take people up or down.
5 A verb that means you're late for a plane and you can't catch it.
6 The door in the airport that takes you to the plane.

9 Match the words in the box with the pictures 1–4.

get on   get off   land   take off

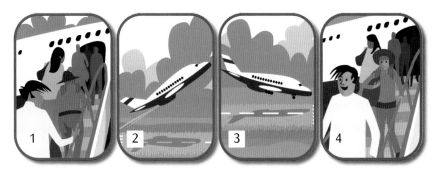

10 Complete the table with all the words from exercises 8 and 9.

The airport	The plane	Documents
escalator	*flight attendant*	*passport*

11 Complete the text with words from the table in exercise 10.

I gave the check-in assistant my (1) … . The check-in assistant gave me a (2) … . Then I went up the (3) … to passport control and showed my (4) … . I was late. I had twenty minutes to (5) … my plane. I ran because I didn't want to (6) … the plane. I was the last passenger to arrive at (7) … 22.

 WORKBOOK PAGES 29, 32

TALK ABOUT IT

1 Do you know any stories about travel and adventures?
2 What is your favourite thing about an adventure book or film you like? What happens?

Grammar

Past simple Regular Verbs

1 🔊 **What does the photo show? Where do you think they took it? Read the text quickly and check your answers.**

History books say that man arrived on the moon on 20th July 1969. Three astronauts travelled on the spaceship *Apollo 11*: Neil Armstrong, Ed Aldrin and Michael Collins. Armstrong and Aldrin walked on the moon, but Collins didn't leave the *Apollo.*

But did these men travel in space? Some people say that *Apollo 11* didn't go to the moon. They say someone made a film of Armstrong and Aldrin in a studio. So why did somebody make the film?

2 **Look at the photo. Did *Apollo 11* go to the moon or was it a fraud? What do you think?**

3 **Look at the rule and the sentence. Find two more examples of the past simple affirmative in the text.**

> We use the past simple to talk about an event that finished in the past.
> *Man **arrived** on the moon on 20th July 1969.*

4 **Look at the rules. Then look at the text on page 38. Find a past simple affirmative example of each type of verb A–D.**

A	To form the past simple of most regular verbs, we add *-ed* (*start – started*).
B	Verbs ending in *-e*, we add *-d* (*love – loved*).
C	Verbs ending in consonant + *-y*, we remove the *-y* and add *-ied* (*study – studied*).
D	Verbs ending in one vowel and one consonant, we double the consonant and add *-ed* (*stop – stopped*).

5 **Complete the sentences with the past simple affirmative of the verbs in brackets.**

1 Last year I … very hard for my exams. (work)
2 Yesterday we … for hours. (walk)
3 She … because she was late. (hurry)
4 I lost my passport when I … my bag. (drop)
5 Last night I … my favourite film. (watch)
6 He … a lot for his new play. (rehearse)

Past simple Irregular verbs

6 **Match the irregular verbs 1–10 with the past simple forms a–j.**

1	speak	a	forgot
2	tell	b	lost
3	lose	c	spoke
4	go	d	had
5	have	e	learnt
6	eat	f	thought
7	learn	g	ate
8	think	h	made
9	make	i	told
10	forget	j	went

Quick tip Turn to page 119 and look at the list of irregular verbs. Try to learn the past simple form of a few verbs every day!

7 **Write the past simple form of the verbs 1–9.**

1	meet	4	do	7	know
2	come	5	read	8	drink
3	break	6	put	9	leave

8 **Complete the sentences with the past simple form of the verbs in brackets.**

1 My dad … the bus in the city centre and … at the sports centre. (get on / get off)
2 We … a lot of hamburgers in New York. (eat)
3 She … the train at 10 p.m. (catch)
4 We … a famous actor at the theatre. (see)
5 He … in the London marathon last year. (run)
6 The plane was late. It … at midnight! (take off)
7 I … a book to read on the plane. (bring)

Past simple Negatives and questions

9 Look at the rule and the example sentences.

> We use *didn't* + infinitive to make negative sentences in the past simple.
> *Collins didn't leave the Apollo.*
> *Apollo 11 didn't go to the moon.*

10 Correct three mistakes in the email. Find the facts in exercise 1. Then listen and check.

From Sam@highscore.com
Date Wednesday, 20 January
To Gill@highscore.com

Hi Gill,

Here's some information for our project on space.
~~Apollo 11 went to Mars~~ on 20th July 1969. Collins walked *Apollo 11 didn't go to Mars. It went to the moon!*
on the moon. Armstrong and Aldrin stayed on the
Apollo. Some people say it didn't happen! They made a
film of Armstrong and Aldrin in the desert!

See you later,

Sam

11 Look at the rule and the questions.

> We use *did* + infinitive to make questions in the past simple.
> *Did these men travel in space?*
> *Why did somebody make the film?*

12 Write past simple questions.

1 did / What / buy? / you
2 read? / he / did / Which book
3 they / meet friends / Did / on Saturday?
4 her friends / Did? / she / visit
5 miss / he / Did / the train?
6 arrive? / When / they / did

13 Write past simple questions for the answers.

1 We went to San Francisco.
2 Yes, we caught a plane.
3 We went with our parents.
4 We stayed at a hotel in the centre of San Francisco.
5 Yes, we had a good time.
6 No, we didn't buy any souvenirs.

Consolidation

14 Complete the dialogue with the past simple form of the verbs in brackets. Listen and check.

Into the blue: Chapter three

Dave Hey, look through the window.
Suzy Why is it so dark? It's only two o'clock!
Dave I don't know.
Suzy Dave, … you … (1 see) that passenger?
Dave Which passenger? The one that
 … (2 speak) to the flight attendant?
Suzy Yes. His hands! He … (3 have) hands like
 the skin of a fish!
Dave Where … you … (4 buy) the tickets?
Suzy I … (5 not buy) them, I … (6 win) them in a
 competition on the internet.
Dave What … you … (7 answer) questions
 about in the competition?
Suzy The legend of Atlantis. I … (8 study) it.
 We … (9 do) a project on Atlantis at
 school.

Dave … (10 look) through the window again.
He … (11 see) strange lights, like the lights of a
big city.

Voice We're landing in five minutes. Please
 have your swimming costumes ready.
Suzy Why do we need swimming costumes?
Dave They … (12 not tell) you everything in that
 competition. I think we're learning even
 more about Atlantis!

 GRAMMAR REFERENCE PAGE 105
WORKBOOK PAGE 30

Communication

Vocabulary Prepositions of movement

1 **What was the flight attendant's route to work? Complete the sentences with the words in the box.**

under   through   over   down   across   up

She went (1) … the stairs. She went (2) … the door. She went (3) … the bridge. She went (4) … the road. She went (5) … the bridge. She went (6) … the escalator.

Listening A lost camera

2 **Look at the pictures. What do you think is happening?**

3 **Listen. Put the pictures a–d into the correct order.**

1 …   2 …   3 …   4 …

4 **Listen again. Choose the correct answer.**

1 They arrived at the airport 13 / 30 / 35 minutes before the plane took off.
2 Maria **had** / **didn't have** a good time.
3 Did Maria buy any souvenirs?
   Yes / No / We don't know
4 Mike / the flight attendant helped Maria on the plane.
5 Mike / the flight attendant had Maria's camera.

Speaking Travel

5 **In pairs, read the dialogue.**

A Where did you go for your last holiday?
B I went to Berlin.
A Who did you travel with?
B I went with my family.
A Did you travel by plane?

6 **Make up a dialogue about your last holiday. Act out your dialogue in class.**

 WORKBOOK PAGE 32

Culture focus

1 Which country do you think these photos are from?
What do you think the boy is doing?

Tanami desert

2 🔊 Read the text and check your ideas.

WALKABOUT

What did you do for your last birthday? Did you have a party? Did you go out with your friends or family? Well, on the day of his thirteenth birthday, Jangala from Central Australia walked around the Tanami desert for a week, and he did it alone!

Jangala didn't take any food with him to eat in the desert; he ate the small animals and snakes he caught with his boomerang and spear. He made small fires to cook his food, and at night he slept under the stars on the desert floor. In fact, Jangala showed he was a good Warlpiri.

The Warlpiri people have modern lives like most people in Australia, but they also have their own traditions. One of these traditions is *Walkabout*, the moment when a boy becomes an adult. When a boy is thirteen, he leaves his family and travels on foot around the desert. In this way, he shows that he can survive.

After a week Jangala returned, and his family celebrated his new status. Jangala was obviously happy. Firstly because he was now an adult, and secondly because not long ago Warlpiri boys usually spent 6 months on *Walkabout*!

3 Answer the questions.

1 What did Jangala do on his thirteenth birthday?
2 How did Jangala show he was a good Warlpiri?
3 Do you think the Warlpiri people have old-fashioned lives?
4 What new status does a Warlpiri boy have when he finishes *Walkabout*?
5 When did Jangala come back from *Walkabout*?
6 Is *Walkabout* easier now for Warlpiri boys? Why?

TALK ABOUT IT

1 What important events happen in the life of a boy or girl in your country?

2 What was the last family celebration you went to?

Writing

A postcard Ordering events

1 **Read the postcard. Choose the correct answers.**

Dear Jane,
We're having a great time in New York!
    We saw all the famous places on Monday on a tourist bus. It was a very long day!
    (1) **Firstly / After that**, we went to the Empire State building and (2) **finally / then** we walked around Central Park. (3) **Next / first of all**, the bus took us down Fifth Avenue. (4) **After that / At the end**, we got off at the Statue of Liberty. (5) **Next / Finally**, we saw the famous Brooklyn Bridge and we went to the hotel. I took a lot of photos of everything.
    There are so many things to see!
    See you soon,
    Sara

Jane Smith
1 The Street
Brighton
BN1 ABC
U.K.

2 **Complete the table with words from the postcard.**

Words to start	What happened next	Words to finish
Firstly		

3 **Make notes for a postcard to a friend. Think about these things:**

- Where are you? Are you having a good time?
- What did you do? When?
- What did you see?
- Did you catch a plane, a bus, a train, etc.?
- Did you take photos?

4 **Write your postcard. Remember to:**

- use the words from exercise 2 to order the events.
- start *Dear* (friend's name) and finish with your name.
- check your work, especially the past simple irregular verbs.

 WORKBOOK PAGE 33

Quick check

Vocabulary

1 Do the vocabulary quiz.

1 What is the opposite of *catch* a plane, bus or train?

2 Who works on a plane?
a a flight attendant
b a check-in assistant

3 What is the opposite of *get on* a plane, bus or train?

4 Which document does a check-in assistant give you?
a a ticket
b a passport
c a boarding card

5 What does a plane do first:
a land   b take off?

6 Which airport door do you walk through to get on a plane?

2 Complete the text with the words in the box.

miss   flight attendant   boarding card   ticket
gate   escalator

My return journey from Amsterdam was a disaster! I couldn't find my (1) … ! The check-in assistant said I couldn't catch the plane. In the end, she gave me a replacement. Finally I got my (2) … and I ran up the (3) … and went through passport control. I only had five minutes to find (4) … 55! I didn't (5) … my plane because it was late. The (6) … showed me my seat. Then the plane took off. I opened my book and there was my ticket!

Vocabulary review: Units 1–4

3 Choose the correct answer.

1 In the evenings I … the internet.
   a navigate   b go on
2 I think soaps are good. My favourite, *Heart of the City*, is really … .
   a brilliant   b terrible
3 Actors … a lot before the first performance.
   a rehearse   b perform
4 She doesn't do any work. She's very … .
   a lazy   b selfish
5 I want to go on a … because I always know the answers to the questions.
   a documentary   b quiz show

Grammar

4 Complete the table in the past simple.

Affirmative	Negative
He liked sport.	(1) …
(2) …	They didn't speak to me.
I studied maths.	(3) …
(4) …	You didn't go up the stairs.
The train stopped.	(5) …
(6) …	She didn't eat pasta.

5 Write questions about last weekend.

1 weekend? / go / did / last / Where / you
2 go / the / you / cinema? / Did / to
3 Saturday? / wear / on / did / you / What
4 you / on / Where / Sunday / were / morning ?
5 at / mum / out / the / your / weekend? / Did / go out
6 see / your / friend? / you / best / did
7 time / to / on / What / you / did / bed / Sunday? / go
8 homework? / Did / do / you / your

6 Answer your questions from exercise 5. Write sentences in the past simple.

Grammar review: Units 1–4

7 There are mistakes in six of the sentences. Find the mistakes and correct them.

1 When I was younger I could swim but now I swim every day.
2 Which is the better football team in the world?
3 We was very happy after the exam.
4 She always goes to the cinema on Fridays.
5 The students didn't do their homework and the teacher was angry with they.
6 Soaps are more interesting than sports programmes.
7 My dad goes sometimes to work at the weekends.
8 Were she at school yesterday?

Reading

1 Why do you think the girl in the photo is a hero?

2 Read the text and check your ideas.

YOUNG HEROES

Bethany Hamilton

On October 31st 2003, Bethany Hamilton went surfing at a beach in Hawaii. The weather was perfect, but suddenly some sharks appeared. There were other people in the water nearby but they couldn't help her. A shark attacked her and bit off her left arm.

Did Bethany stop surfing? Not at all! A month after leaving hospital, thirteen-year-old Bethany was in the sea again because she was determined to surf. Now Bethany surfs for the USA National Team and she also collects money to help disabled children all around the world.

Iqbal Massih and Craig Kielburger

Twelve-year-old Iqbal Massih worked in a factory, so he told the world about the children's terrible conditions in Pakistan. Then, in 1995, someone killed him. Another twelve year-old, Craig Kielburger, read about Iqbal. Craig suddenly understood that a young person can make a difference.

Craig visited Pakistan and he saw the children's awful conditions. Then he wrote a book about how the children worked all day in factories and never went to school. He also started an organisation, *Free The Children*. Some schools and his local town hall helped him. They collected some money to buy food, pencils and paper and to build schools in 300 villages. Craig now thinks Iqbal didn't die in vain.

Brandon Keefe

Brandon Keefe had a brilliant idea for his secondary school community project. Did his classmates have any old books at home that they didn't want? There was a local orphanage that didn't have any books. Brandon could give the books to the orphanage to create a library.

Brandon collected 5,000 books from friends and book shops, so he began an organisation called *BookEnds*. *BookEnds* gave 150,000 books to 46 children's libraries. Brandon didn't like reading before, but he loves reading now!

3 Which of the four people is your favourite young hero? Why?

4 Choose the correct answer.

1 After leaving hospital, Bethany …
   a soon surfed again.
   b didn't surf for months.
2 Bethany now collects money for …
   a children with physical problems.
   b surfers.
3 Thanks to the story about Iqbal…
   a *Free The Children* built a village.
   b Craig started to help poor children.
4 Craig wrote a book …
   a after he visited Pakistan.
   b before he visited Pakistan.
5 Brandon's community project …
   a gave books to his friends.
   b found books for children to read.
6 Now Brandon feels …
   a different about reading.
   b the same about reading.

5 What do these dates and numbers in the text represent?

1 5,000   3 13   5 46
2 31st   4 300   6 1995

6 Match the sentences 1–5 with the four heroes in the text.

1 His / Her friends gave him / her something. *Brandon*
2 He / She worked in bad conditions.
3 He / She didn't stop his / her favourite activity.
4 He / She began an organisation.
5 He / She wrote a book.

7 Answer the questions.

1 What did Craig suddenly realise?
2 Who didn't go to school?
3 Where did Bethany go surfing?
4 What does Bethany now do for her country?
5 Who didn't have any books?

Vocabulary Town and city

8 Find a place in the box where …

town hall   cinema   book shop   stadium   library
museum   hospital   car park   fire station   secondary school
train station   factory

1 you study when you're a teenager.
2 you go if you have an accident.
3 you buy books.
4 the local government is.
5 you borrow books.
6 people and machines make products.
7 you visit and look at important, old things.
8 you leave your car.
9 you watch a film.
10 you watch a football match.
11 you catch a train.
12 the people work who stop fires and help in dangerous situations.

9 Complete the text with words from exercise 8.

I live in Liverpool, a big city in the north of England. There are so many things to do! I often watch films at the (1) … . There is a big art gallery and there are lots of (2) … with fascinating things to see. On Saturdays we go to watch Liverpool play football at the (3) … . I love reading and there are lots of good (4) … . However, I haven't got much money to buy books, but there is also a big (5) … – I usually borrow three books from there a week.

10 Match the people 1–7 with the places they work a–g.

1 doctors and nurses   a secondary school
2 the mayor   b book shop
3 librarian   c fire station
4 shop assistant   d town hall
5 pupils and teachers   e hospital
6 workers   f factory
7 firefighters   g library

 WORKBOOK PAGES 35,38

TALK ABOUT IT

1 What is a hero? What heroes have you got? Are they famous?
2 What qualities do your heroes have? Write a list of qualities and compare with your partner.

Grammar

Past simple revision

1 How can dogs help people? What jobs do dogs sometimes do?

2 🔘 Read the text. How did Norman help someone?

> You probably know that dogs have good noses, but did you know that they can hear better than humans? Last week Norman, a Labrador, went for a walk with the Barret family by the river Shannon in Ireland. Suddenly, Norman left the Barrets and ran down to the river. Why did he leave the Barrets? Well, Norman could hear something in the water and he didn't wait for the humans to hear it! In the river there was a thirteen-year-old girl, Lisa Bingby. Lisa was in danger. Norman didn't think about the danger, and he swam to Lisa. She caught his tail and Norman pulled her to the side of the river. Now Norman is Lisa's hero!

3 Complete the rule.

> We use ... + ... to make negative sentences in the past simple.

4 Find two past simple negative sentences in the text from exercise 2.

5 Complete the dialogue with the correct past simple form of the verbs in brackets.

Phil	Did you read about that dog that went for a walk by the sea?
Dara	No, it ... (1 not go) for a walk by the sea. It was by the river Shannon.
Phil	Ah yes, and the dog saw a girl in danger.
Dara	No! He ... (2 not see) a girl in danger. He ... (3 hear) a girl in danger!
Phil	That's it! Then a family swam into the river to help the girl.
Dara	No, a family ... (4 not swim) into the river. It was the dog!
Phil	Did the girl pull the dog to the side of the river?
Dara	No, Phil. The girl ... (5 not pull) the dog! The dog ... (6 pull) the girl!
Phil	I think we're talking about two different stories!

6 Complete the rule.

> We use ... + ... to make questions in the past simple.

7 Find two past simple questions in the text from exercise 2.

8 Complete the past simple questions for the answers.

When *did Norman go for a walk?*
Norman went for a walk last week.

1 Who ... ?
Norman left the Barrets.

2 Who ... ?
Norman found Lisa Bingby.

3 What ... ?
Lisa caught Norman's tail.

4 Who ... ?
Norman pulled Lisa to the side of the river.

Countable and uncountable nouns

9 Complete the table with the words in the box.
Use the text on page 46 to help you.

~~pencil~~ beach ~~money~~ organisation weather
water factory school village food

Countable nouns	Uncountable nouns
pencil	*money*

10 Complete the text about Craig's visit to Pakistan with *a*, *an*, *some* or *any*.

When we went to Pakistan we had (1) … good weather but it also rained a lot. I visited (2) … organisation that helped (3) … villages. The people in the villages didn't have (4) … money to buy food. Their children worked in (5) … factory in the village. Did I see (6) … schools in the village? No! The people didn't have (7) … pencils and they didn't have (8) … paper. There was nothing to help them study. The factory was terrible. The children worked for ten hours a day. There was (9) … food and water in the factory, but it wasn't for the children – it was for the adults. These children never studied or played! I wanted to help so I wrote (10) … book about the children.

11 Match the rules A–D with the sentences 1–4.

	Countable nouns
A	We use *a / an / some* with countable nouns in affirmative sentences.
B	We use *any* with countable nouns in negative sentences and questions.
	Uncountable nouns
C	We use *some* with uncountable nouns in affirmative sentences.
D	We use *any* with uncountable nouns in negative sentences and questions.

1 We had some good weather.
2 The people in the villages didn't have any money.
3 Their children worked in a factory in the village.
4 Did I see any schools in the village?

12 Choose the correct answer.

1 Did Bethany see **any / some** sharks?
2 The schools collected **some / a** money.
3 Brandon's friends gave him **any / some** books.
4 There wasn't **any / a** food in the villages.
5 They didn't have **any / a** houses.

Consolidation

13 Complete the text with the past simple form of the verbs. When there is no verb, use *some* or *any*.

Last year there … (1 be) lots of films about super heroes, but real heroes are more interesting! Craig … (2 go) to Pakistan to help children and he … (3 start) organisation. How … a twelve-year-old boy … (4 begin) an organisation? He … (5 have) the help of (6) … school friends in Canada. At first, there weren't (7) … people from other countries in the organisation. When they started, they … (8 not have) any money so they … (9 create) friendship schools. The organisation didn't have (10) … problems finding schools in North America and Europe that … (11 want) to help. Today, more than one million children help *Free the children*.

GRAMMAR REFERENCE PAGE 106
WORKBOOK PAGE 36

Communication

Vocabulary -ed and -ing adjectives

1 Which sentence is about how a person feels? Which sentence describes a thing or a person?

1 I'm *interested* in super heroes.
2 Some TV documentaries are very *interesting*.

2 Choose the correct answer.

1 Superhero comics are very **interested / interesting**.
2 Watching TV is **bored / boring**.
3 I'm **frightened / frightening** of spiders.
4 Today is Kim's birthday. She's **excited / exciting**.
5 Today is 10 August and it's snowing. It's very **surprised / surprising**.
6 My Mum is very **worried / worrying** because I am late.
7 I didn't finish the book because I was **bored / boring**.
8 We went to Disneyland. It was **excited / exciting**.
9 We were **surprised / surprising** that Brazil didn't win the match.
10 Horror films are very **frightened / frightening**.

Listening Superheroes

3 Do you know the names of the superheroes 1–4? What powers do they have? Which is your favourite?

4 Listen to the radio programme. Choose the correct answer.

1 Stan Lee wrote the first Spider-Man stories in …
   a 1972.   b 1962.   c 1982.
2 Peter Parker became an orphan when he was …
   a seven.   b sixteen.   c six.
3 Peter Parker went to live with his …
   a sister.   b granddad. c uncle and aunt.
4 A radioactive spider bit Peter's …
   a hand.   b ear.   c arm.
5 Spider-Man is very popular because he …
   a has super powers and astonishing problems.
   b has the same problems we all have in normal life.
   c uses his powers in normal situations.

5 Listen again. Which adjective do you hear?

1 surprised / surprising   4 worried / worrying
2 bored / boring   5 excited / exciting
3 frightened / frightening 6 interested / interesting

Speaking A day out

6 In pairs, read the dialogue.

7 Make up a dialogue about a place you visited at the weekend. Act out your dialogue in class.

> A Where did you go at the weekend?
> B I went to the museum with my parents. There was an Egyptian exhibition.
> C Did you have a good time?
> D I had a great time. It was very exciting!

WORKBOOK PAGE 38

Culture focus

A

B

C

1 **Look at the photos and discuss the questions.**

What do you know about cowboys?

Where do you think they came from?

2 💿 **Read the text and check your ideas.**

HEROES OF THE WILD WILD WEST

1 History

The Spanish introduced cowboy culture to America 500 years ago. The image of the cowboy is popular today because of Hollywood films, but real cowboys were different. About 40% of cowboys were African Americans and Native Americans. When president Abraham Lincoln stopped slavery on January 1st 1863, lots of African Americans became cowboys, because they could travel freely for the first time. Many Native Americans also became cowboys in the nineteenth century. The Indian wars destroyed the Native Americans' culture, so many of them became cowboys to survive.

2 Gunfighters

There were three types of cowboy gunfighters. Some worked on ranches and protected them against other gunfighters. Others were criminals and they attacked travellers and robbed banks. Finally, the third group were sheriffs: Wild West policemen. Gunfighters' lives were very exciting, but most cowboys weren't gunfighters.

3 Today

Cowboys continue to look after cows, but now they use modern technology. Therefore, their lives are easier. On the big ranches cowboys use satellite cameras, so they can see where their cows are. They follow the cows in large ranch cars, because they are quicker and more comfortable. Life is better, but they continue to get up at 5 a.m. or 6 a.m. and work until the sun goes down!

3 **Match the paragraphs 1-3 with the photos A-C.**

4 **Answer the questions.**

1 Why is the image of the cowboy well known today?
2 How many cowboys were African Americans and Native Americans?
3 What did the gunfighters on ranches do?
4 Who did the criminals attack? What else did they do?
5 How is life easier for cowboys today?

TALK ABOUT IT

1 Which heroes are there in your country?
2 What do they do? Why are they heroes?

Writing

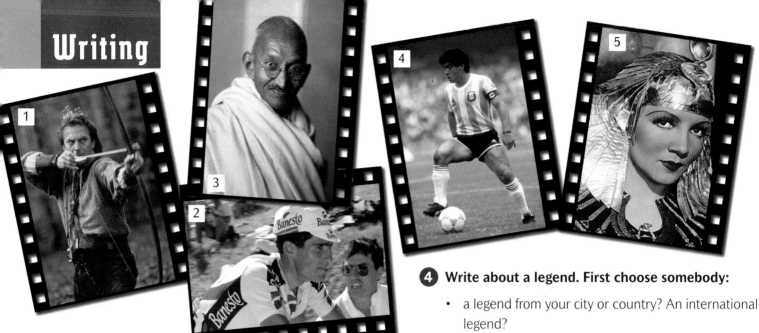

Writing about a legend

because and *so*

1 **Who are the people in the photos 1–5? What do you know about them?**

2 **Look at the rules and the example sentences.**

Action + *because* + reason *I ate an apple because I was hungry.*
Reason + *so* + action *I was hungry, so I ate an apple.*

3 **Complete the text with *so* or *because*.**

Robin Hood lived 700 years ago in Sherwood Forest, England. At that time, the people were very poor. Robin became famous (1) … he attacked rich travellers and took their money. Then he gave the money to the poor people, (2) … the poor people loved him. But the Sheriff of Nottingham wanted to catch Robin (3) … the Sheriff's rich friends were unhappy.

The King of England, Richard I, wasn't in the country then, (4) … his bad brother, Prince John, wanted to become king. Robin and his men stopped Prince John (5) … they were strong and brave and they loved their country.

Robin Hood died in 1247. He didn't die in the forest. He went to stay in a small village (6) … he wasn't well. He is still a legend 700 years later and we continue to talk about him.

4 **Write about a legend. First choose somebody:**

- a legend from your city or country? An international legend?
- in your family, e.g. a grandparent?

Now look for information and make notes.

5 **Organise your information.**

Paragraph 1: Who was he /she? Where did he / she live? When did he / she live? What did he / she do?

Paragraph 2: More examples of the things he /she did.

Paragraph 3: When did he / she die or finish his / her activity? What happened?

6 **Write about the legend. Remember to:**

- use *so* to say what happened after your legend did something.
- use *because* to explain why your legend did something.
- check that the past simple verb forms are correct.

Quick tip Use the phrases in the box to help you write your sentences.

He / She (lived / acted / sang / played football etc.)
(number) years ago.
At that time, (pop music was very boring) …
He / She was famous because …
The people loved him / her but …
He / She died / stopped (playing football / acting)
in (year) …
… (number) years later he / she is a legend and
we continue to talk about him / her.

 WORKBOOK PAGE 39

Quick check

Vocabulary

1 Where do you find these people? Write the names of the places.

1	a librarian	4	the mayor
2	a firefighter	5	a doctor
3	a pupil	6	workers

2 Where can you …

1 find help when there's a fire?
2 buy books?
3 go when you are ill?
4 watch a film?
5 park your car?
6 look at very old, interesting things?
7 watch football?
8 get on a train?

3 Choose the correct answer.

1 The film was **bored** / **boring**. I went to sleep!
2 She's very **interested** / **interesting** in music.
3 Spider-Man is very shy. That's **surprised** / **surprising**!
4 My mum is **frightened** / **frightening** of snakes.
5 Last week we had a football match. It was very **excited** / **exciting**.
6 I've got two exams this afternoon and I'm very **worried** / **worrying**!

Vocabulary review: Units 1–5

4 Answer the questions.

1 Which verb means a plane goes up into the sky?
   a take off **b** land
2 Which person helps friends with problems?
   a a sympathetic person **b** a moody person
3 Which words are similar?

funny	hilarious
frightening	wonderful
bad	terrifying
good	awful

4 Name two things you wear to play sport.
5 Do you *do* or *play* gymnastics?

Grammar

5 Complete the table.

Infinitive	Past simple
be	(1) …
(2) …	became
catch	(3) …
(4) …	came
give	(5) …
(6) …	went
have	(7) …
(8) …	saw

6 Write affirmative and negative sentences and questions in the past simple. Use the verbs in the box.

become   write   give   study   ~~go~~   bite

Mike / to the cinema **?**
Did Mike go to the museum?

1 They / science at school yesterday ✗
2 Craig / a book about Iqbal ?
3 Native Americans / cowboys ✓
4 The snake / you ✗
5 The students / us some pens and paper ✓

7 Choose the correct answer.

1 Have you got **some** / **any** food?
2 We went to **any** / **a** museum yesterday.
3 We collected **some** / **any** paper.
4 We didn't have **a** / **any** money.
5 There were **some** / **any** books in the library.

Grammar review: Units 1–5

8 There are mistakes in five of the sentences. Find the mistakes and correct them.

1 She didn't goes to the museum.
2 I can run faster five years ago than I can now.
3 My parents don't like watch my DVDs.
4 We don't have some books.
5 They often visit art galleries at the weekends.
6 Mike's house is bigger then your house.

The power of nature

Reading

1 What type of weather caused the damage in the photo? Where does this type of weather happen?

2 Read the text and check your answers.

A REAL GEOGRAPHY LESSON

Tilly Smith, a young school girl from Surrey in England, is very enthusiastic about her geography classes. But on 26 December 2004 Tilly discovered that geography is more than just an interesting school subject. Tilly was sitting on the beach **A** ... in Phuket, Thailand, when the sea suddenly disappeared. What was happening? While big waves were forming, Tilly and the tourists watched. At first, they weren't afraid, but Tilly remembered her geography lessons and she became anxious. She wanted to leave the beach quickly.

At school Tilly studied earthquakes. **B** ... She recognised what was happening, but the other tourists weren't moving from the beach. She was very tense. Tilly told her mother about tectonic plates and an earthquake under the sea. Tilly became very upset. In the end she was desperate to leave the beach with her family.

Tilly's father told the other tourists about the danger, while Tilly was running to a safe place with her mother and sister.

Everybody was running to safety when the first of three tsunami waves came up the beach. When Tilly and the others looked down **C** ..., the waves were destroying the small tourist centre.

After the tsunami, a lot of tourists were grateful for Tilly's interest in geography. Her parents were glad she listened in class **D** ... . The tsunami was a terrible accident for thousands and thousands of people. But, thanks to Tilly, it didn't kill anybody on Maikhao beach.

3 **What type of text is it?**

1 an email to a friend
2 a police report
3 a magazine article

4 **Match the information 1–4 with the spaces A–D in the text.**

1 and they were very proud of her.
2 from safety
3 on Maikhao beach
4 She knew they sometimes cause tsunamis.

5 **Read the text again and order the events.**

a Tilly and the tourists watched the formation of big waves.
b The waves destroyed the tourist centre.
c Tilly Smith studied tsunamis at school.
d The tourists were happy that Tilly likes geography.
e Everybody ran to safety.
f The sea suddenly disappeared.

6 **Are the sentences true or false? Explain your answers.**

1 Tilly was at school on 26 December 2004.
2 Tilly's school geography lessons helped her understand the situation.
3 Tilly's mum explained the situation to her.
4 Tilly's dad ran to safety with his family.
5 Everybody was running to safety when the tsunami arrived.
6 The tsunami killed thousands of people on Maikhao beach.

Vocabulary Adjectives of emotion

7 **Read the text again. Make a list of the adjectives of emotion.**

8 **Match the definitions 1–7 with the adjectives a–g.**

When a person …

1 thanks someone for something,
2 is sad about something,
3 worries about something bad in the future,
4 is frightened about a situation,
5 is happy,
6 is very interested in something,
7 is very worried and wants to change a situation very quickly,

he / she is …

a glad.   e upset.
b desperate.   f afraid.
c enthusiastic.   g grateful.
d anxious.

9 **Find the opposites of the adjectives 1–3 in the text.**

1 ashamed   2 uninterested   3 relaxed

10 **Complete the table with all the adjectives from exercises 8 and 9.**

Positive	Negative
glad	desperate

11 **Choose the correct answer.**

1 Our daughter made us **proud / anxious**. She saved a lot of people.
2 After the terrible experience in Thailand, they were **upset / glad** to go home.
3 I'm very **grateful / tense** for your help.
4 I was **ashamed / proud** when I didn't pass any of my exams.
5 After the tsunami we were **desperate / afraid** to swim again.

 WORKBOOK PAGES 41, 44

TALK ABOUT IT

1 Can you remember a situation when you were anxious or afraid?

2 What happened? When did it happen? Who were you with? What happened in the end?

Grammar

Past continuous Affirmative

1 💿 **Read the text.**

Young Dave McSheffrey was skiing in Colorado, USA when he got lost! Where was he going? He didn't know, but it was important to go down the mountain before night came. Firstly, he skied through the woods until the snow finished. Then he found a river. While he was walking along the river, he saw some bears. Were they looking for a boy to eat? No, they were fishing and they were eating salmon. The bears didn't see him, so Dave continued along the river. He was tired and he couldn't walk fast. Dave was walking slowly when he saw a village on the other side of the river and he found a boat. He was going across the river in the boat when somebody saw him. He was safe!

2 **Look at the rule. Then find two more examples of the past continuous affirmative in the text.**

> We form the past continuous affirmative with subject + *was / were* + *-ing* form.
> **1** *He was walking along the river.*
> **2** ...
> **3** ...

3 **Complete the sentences with the correct past continuous form of the verbs in brackets.**

1 The actors ... a play. (rehearse)
2 Bryony ... her homework. (do)
3 My parents ... in Rome. (stay)
4 I ... to the radio. (listen)
5 Craig ... a book. (write)
6 You ... your grandparents. (visit)

Past continuous
Negatives and questions

4 **Look at the rule and the example sentences.**

> We form the past continuous negative with subject + *wasn't / weren't* + *-ing* form.
> *He wasn't skiing fast.*
> *The other tourists weren't moving from the beach.*

5 **Look at the text from exercise 1. Then correct the mistakes in the newspaper report.**

He wasn't walking. He was skiing.

Young skier safe!

Young Dave McSheffrey got lost in Colorado while he was walking in the mountains.

He skied through the woods and then he walked along a river. While he was fishing he saw some bears. The bears were playing and they were eating honey. Dave continued along the river. Dave was running when he saw a village. He was swimming across the river when somebody saw him from the village.

6 **Look at the rule and the questions.**

> We form past continuous questions with *was / were* + subject + *-ing* form.
> *Where was he skiing?*
> *Were they looking for a boy to eat?*

7 **Write past continuous questions for the answers.**

1 Where / Dave / ski?
   Dave was skiing in Colorado, USA.
2 Where / Dave / walk?
   He was walking along the river.
3 What / the / bears do?
   The bears were fishing.
4 What / the bears / eat?
   The bears were eating salmon.
5 Dave / walk fast?
   No, Dave was walking slowly.
6 Dave / swim across the river?
   No, he was going across the river in a boat.

Past simple or past continuous?

8 Look at the rules and the sentences.

> We use the past continuous to talk about events or actions that were in progress at a specific time in the past.
>
> We use the past simple to talk about events or actions that finished at a specific time in the past.
>
> We often use the past continuous with the past simple. We use the past continuous to talk about a longer action and the past simple with a shorter action that interrupts the longer action.
> *Dave was going across the river when someone saw him.*
> *My mobile rang while I was walking to school.*

9 Complete the sentences with the past simple form of the verb in brackets.

1 Dave … (see) some bears while he was walking along the river.
2 I was doing my homework when someone … (send) me a text message.
3 My parents were living in London when they … (meet).
4 It was raining when we … (leave) school.
5 A shark … (attack) Bethany while she was swimming in the sea.

10 Complete the sentences with the correct past continuous form of the verbs in brackets.

1 Dave McSheffrey … (ski), when he got lost.
2 We … (not work) when the teacher returned to the classroom.
3 … you … (do) your homework when I was at the shops?
4 She didn't watch TV while she … (study) for her exams.
5 I … (not listen) when the teacher asked me a question.
6 … they … (have) lunch when you visited them?
7 My computer crashed while I … (write) an email.
8 … he … (sleep) when you sent him a text message?

Consolidation

11 Complete the text with the past simple or past continuous form of the verbs in brackets. Then listen and check.

Two weeks before her holiday, Tilly Smith's class … (**1** study) earthquakes and volcanoes when her geography teacher, Mr Kearney, told them that earthquakes and volcanoes can cause tsunamis. Tilly … (**2** be) very interested in tsunamis. While Mr Kearney … (**3** teach) the class about tsunamis, he … (**4** explain) that after the sea disappears, the next five to ten minutes are very important for people to survive.

Tilly is now back at school in Surrey, England, after her frightening experience in Thailand. She … (**5** tell) the geography class how she … (**6** see) the sea disappear while she … (**7** sit) on the beach. Thanks to her geography teacher, she knew what to do.

WORKBOOK PAGE 42
GRAMMAR REFERENCE PAGE 106

Communication

Vocabulary Extreme weather

1 Match the words in the box with the pictures 1–7.

> hurricane flood drought tornado storm
> lightning tsunami

Listening Weather quiz

2 How much do you know about the weather?
Do the weather quiz!

1 How fast can a tsunami travel?	**a** 600 km/hour **b** 300 km/hour **c** 800 km/hour
2 Where do you have more chance of seeing tornadoes?	**a** Great Britain **b** China **c** USA
3 When do tornadoes happen? When there is a …	**a** drought? **b** storm? **c** flood?
4 Which happens first?	**a** thunder then lightning **b** lightning then thunder **c** they happen at the same time
5 Hurricanes always begin in the …	**a** mountains. **b** forests. **c** ocean.
6 Which city has the most rain and floods?	**a** Manchester, England **b** Cherraapunji,India **c** Sydney, Australia

3  Listen to the radio programme and check your answers.

4 Listen again. Are the sentences true or false? Explain your answers.

1 Planes are faster than tsunamis.
2 Lightning is made by thunder.
3 Hurricanes start in oceans near the equator.
4 It rains 1,270 cm of water in Cairo a year.

Speaking Weather

5 In pairs, read the dialogue.

> **A** What type of extreme weather happens where you live?
> **B** We sometimes have droughts.
> **A** What do you do when there is a drought?
> **B** Well, we don't make fires. Fires are very dangerous when there's a drought.

6 Make up a dialogue about the weather where you live. Act out your dialogue in class.

➡ WORKBOOK PAGE 44

Culture focus

SD – South Dakota
OK – Oklahoma
TX – Texas

1 Look at the map. Which country is it? What do you think *Tornado Alley* is?

2 Read the text and check your ideas.

TORNADO ALLEY

I discovered tornadoes while I was studying English in Woodward, a town in Oklahoma in the USA. I was staying with the Tinneman family, and everything was perfect until my last week. Gary and I were eating a snack in the garden, when suddenly the sky went black; it was a tornado!

Most tornadoes in the USA happen in Tornado Alley, where Oklahoma is. The Alley is west of the Appalachian Mountains and goes from Texas in the south to South Dakota in the north.

We went into a room under the house. Gary was telling me about tornadoes when suddenly there was an explosion upstairs. I thought it was a bomb, but it was the tornado! Gary thought it was an F5 tornado, the strongest type. An F5 tornado moves at 500 km an hour, and can throw cars as far as 100 metres. It also destroys houses!

When we came out, we saw that the Tinneman's house didn't have a roof or any windows. I was upset for the Tinnemans, but Gary said they were lucky. His friends' houses were completely destroyed.

3 Match the places in the box with 1–3 on the map.

Woodward   the Appalachian Mountains
Tornado Alley

4 Answer the questions.

1 Why was the writer staying in the USA?
2 Why did the sky go black when they were having a snack in the garden?
3 Where do a lot of tornadoes happen in the USA?
4 What type of tornado was it?
5 What damage can an F5 tornado do?
6 Which house didn't have a roof or windows?
7 Why was the writer upset?
8 What was Gary's reaction to the damage? Why?

TALK ABOUT IT

1 Do you like films about natural disasters?
2 Which is your favourite disaster film? What is it about?
3 What happens in the end? Why do you like it?

Writing

A story Adjective order

1 **Do the adjectives in the box describe …**

1 opinions: what people think about something?
2 facts: the nationality, colour, size of something?

> American   hilarious   wonderful   small   awful
> Spanish   young   terrible   blue   brilliant   big
> cool

Opinion	Fact
hilarious	small

2 **Read the rule and the example sentence.**

> **When there are two adjectives, we put the opinion adjective first and the fact adjective second.**
> *She was a wonderful Japanese student.*

3 **Read the text and put the adjectives in the correct order.**

4 **You are going to write about something that happened to you. First think about a school trip, a holiday or a weekend. Was it a good or bad experience?**

5 **Make notes about these questions.**

- When did it happen?
- Who did you go with?
- How did you travel?
- Where did you go?
- What happened?
- What were you doing when it happened?

6 **Write your story. Remember to:**

- use some adjectives to describe the journey, the place and what happened.
- put the adjectives you use in the correct order.

WORKBOOK PAGE 45

A weekend to remember!

Last year we went camping for the first and last time! We set off in dad's … (1 **fantastic / new**) car at 8 a.m. and we arrived in Cornwall six hours later. Cornwall is a … (2 **green / beautiful**) part of England, but it's got a problem - the … (3 **English / awful**) weather!

That first night we went to sleep in our … (4 **wonderful / big**) tent, but while we were sleeping, a storm woke us up. It was very frightening and we left the tent and went to the car. Suddenly, while we were running to the car, the sky became an … (5 **yellow / incredible**) colour; it was lightning. Then, there was an explosion and a tree fell onto our tent!

We were all very upset and we stayed in the car all night. The next morning we went to a hotel. After our … (6 **horrible / stormy**) night, I thought it was the best hotel in the world!

Quick check

Vocabulary

① **Choose the correct answers.**

Yesterday I had a maths exam and I was very
(1) ashamed / tense. Then, when the exam finished I
became (2) anxious / glad about next week's exams!
My sister is worse. She is (3) afraid / enthusiastic of
exams. Yesterday she forgot her bag and when she
arrived at the exam she was (4) proud / desperate.
She didn't have a pen! Luckily, her best friend gave her
one. My sister was very (5) uninterested / grateful.

② **Choose the correct answer.**

1 What do we call a strong wind that begins in the
   ocean?
   a a tsunami   b a hurricane
2 When does thunder happen? When there's a …
   a storm   b tornado
3 What happens before thunder?
   a a tornado   b lightning
4 What happens when it doesn't rain for a long time?
   a an earthquake   b a drought
5 What happens when it rains a lot?
   a a flood   b a drought
6 What can move cars 100 metres?
   a a drought   b a tornado
7 What do we call very, very big waves?
   a a tsunami   b a hurricane

Vocabulary review: Units 1–6

③ **Complete the sentences with the words in
the box.**

firefighters fascinating necklace frightened
dress hilarious friendly anxious

1 The comedy programme was …!
2 My parents are … of planes. They become … when
   they arrive at the airport.
3 Jane is interested in history and she thinks history
   books are … .
4 When there's a drought the … are prepared for
   dangerous situations.
5 She wore a long … and a gold … .
6 He always smiles and says *hello*. He's very … .

Grammar

④ **Write affirmative or negative sentences or
questions in the past continuous. Use the verbs in
the box.**

destroy ski paint ~~live~~ wear study swim

you / live in New York ?
Were you living in New York?

1 They / jeans yesterday ✗
2 My parents / the house last Saturday ✓
3 a tornado / the city ?
4 she / in the sea ✗
5 I / for the exam ✓
6 your friends / in the mountains ?

⑤ **Complete the sentences with the past simple or
past continuous form of the verbs in brackets.**

1 I … (watch) TV when she … (phone) me.
2 While we … (sit) on the beach, it … (start) to rain.
3 They … (do) their homework when their dad …
   (come) home.
4 I … (eat) a pizza while she … (listen) to her MP3
   player.
5 She … (see) an accident while she … (walk) down
   the street.
6 The train … (stop) six times while we … (travel)
   to London.

Grammar review: Units 1–6

⑥ **Complete the sentences with the words in the box.**

any loves does couldn't were did

1 She … going to the cinema with her friends.
2 … you go to the museum last week?
3 The weather was bad so we … play tennis.
4 Have you got … money?
5 What … he usually eat for breakfast?
6 We … in London last weekend.

Revision: Units 4-6

Vocabulary

1 **Match the words 1–6 with a–f to make phrases.**

1	check-in	a	on
2	boarding	b	attendant
3	take	c	off
4	passport	d	assistant
5	get	e	card
6	flight	f	control

2 **Choose the correct answers.**

1 We didn't want to **miss / catch** the plane so we ran **up / over** the escalator.
2 We went **through / under** the gate and got **on / got off** the plane.
3 He ran **under / across** the road and **through / up** the airport door.
4 The plane **took off / landed** and we got **on / got off**.

3 **Match the people with the descriptions.**

the mayor   doctors and nurses   pupils
firefighters   shop assistant

1 We stop fires and help when there are car accidents.
2 We look after our patients.
3 We study all day.
4 I help people when they buy things.
5 I'm the most important person of a town or city.

4 **Match these places with the people in exercise 3.**

1	town hall	3	fire station	5	hospital
2	shop	4	school		

5 **Choose the correct answer.**

1 I think these photos are very **interested / interesting**.
2 I'm **frightened / frightening** of travelling by plane.
3 My dad has got a new job and he is very **excited / exciting**.
4 I'm at the dentist's. I'm very **worried / worrying**.
5 The internet is very **interested / interesting**.
6 The tornado was very **frightened / frightening**.
7 I was very **surprised / surprising** when I met you in Moscow.
8 Horror films are **bored / boring**.

6 **The adjectives are in the wrong sentences. Change them.**

1 I was very **desperate**. I thanked her for her help.
2 Mike is **glad**. He lost 300 euros in the street.
3 Their sister won three gold medals at the Olympics. They were **afraid** of her.
4 They really like computers and they're very **relaxed** about the internet.
5 They were really **upset** when they passed the exams.
6 He doesn't like swimming. He's **grateful** of the water.
7 We were **enthusiastic**. We were in a taxi, with only fifteen minutes to catch our plane!
8 After her holiday she was very **proud**.

7 **Complete the sentences with the words in the box.**

hurricane   flood   drought   tornado
storm   lightning   tsunami

1 When it doesn't rain for a long time, there is a… .
2 When there are a lot of clouds, lightning and thunder, there is a… .
3 … is the electricity made by a storm.
4 When it rains a lot, there is sometimes a… .
5 A … is a very big wave that can destroy towns and cities.
6 A … moves trees and cars and can destroy houses.
7 A … is a strong wind that begins in the ocean.

Grammar

1 **Put the verbs in the correct column for the past simple form.**

work   study   stop   try   rob   start   rehearse
love   drop   arrive   watch   dry   laugh   like

+*ed*	+*d*	remove *y* +*ied*	double consonant +*ed*

2 **Write sentences about what Julia did last weekend.**

	Morning	Afternoon	Evening
Friday	–	study / at school	rehearse / the school play
Saturday	watch / TV	play / tennis with her sister	try / Indian food
Sunday	travel / to London	visit / an art gallery	return / home

On Friday afternoon she studied at school.

1   On Friday evening … .
2   On Saturday morning … .
3   On Saturday afternoon … .
4   On Saturday evening … .
5   On Sunday morning … .
6   On Sunday afternoon … .
7   On Sunday evening … .

3 **Complete the table.**

Infinitive	Past simple
(1) …	thought
eat	**(2)** …
(3) …	forgot
leave	**(4)** …
(5) …	went
have	**(6)** …
(7) …	spoke
learn	**(8)** …
(9) …	put
tell	**(10)** …

4 **Write negative sentences in the past simple. Use the verbs in the box.**

win   write   walk   paint   sing   see

1   Michael Collins / on the moon.
2   Tilly Smith / *Hamlet.*
3   Picasso / a lot of pictures.
4   Brazil / the World Cup in 1998.
5   I / you yesterday.
6   They / a song at the concert.

5 **Complete the questions in the past simple.**

When *did Apollo 11 leave the Earth*?
Apollo 11 left the Earth on 16th July 1969.
1   Where… ?
   Apollo 11 went to the moon.
2   How long… ?
   Apollo 11 spent nine days in space.
3   What … ?
   Armstrong and Aldrin put a US flag on the moon.
4   What … ?
   Armstrong, Aldrin and Collins wore spacesuits.
5   What… ?
   They brought Moon rocks back to Earth.

6 Complete the sentences with the nouns in the box, then decide if they are countable or uncountable.

money ~~pencil~~ organisation water
school food

I prefer writing with a *pencil. (countable)*

1 Have you got any… ? I want to buy a magazine.
2 My … has got computers in all the classrooms.
3 We bought some … for dinner.
4 There isn't any … in the swimming pool.
5 Craig started an … to help the children in Pakistan.

7 Complete the spaces with *a*, *an*, *some* and *any*.

My favourite place is my bedroom. There's (1) …
computer on my desk. I've also got (2) … computer
games and an MP3 player. But I do other things in my
bedroom. For example, I study! I've got (3) … pens,
(4) … paper and a lot of school books on my desk.
But this weekend I'm really happy because we haven't
got (5) … homework to do! I decorated my bedroom
with (6) … music posters, but I haven't got (7) …
football posters.

8 Complete the sentences in the past continuous.

	Robbie	Ann	Sally
7:00am	do homework	have breakfast	get up
8:00am	cycle to school	cycle to school	leave home
2:00pm	play basketball	do gymnastics	do gymnastics
9:00pm	study for an exam	watch a DVD	study for an exam

Maria *was getting up* at 7 a.m.
1 Robbie … at 7 a.m.
2 Ann … at 7 a.m.
3 Robbie and Ann … at 8 a.m.
4 Sally … at 8 a.m.
5 Ann and Sally … at 2 p.m.
6 Robbie … at 2 p.m.
7 Ann … at 9 p.m.
8 Robbie and Sally … at 9 p.m.

9 Look at the table in exercise 8. Write negative past continuous sentences about Robbie, Ann and Sally.

Sally / do homework at 7 a.m.
Sally wasn't doing homework at 7 a.m.
1 Ann / have breakfast at 8 a.m.
2 Robbie / sleep at 7 a.m.
3 Robbie and Ann / leave home at 8 a.m.
4 Sally cycle to school at 8 a.m.
5 Robbie / do gymnastics at 2p.m.
6 Robbie / play basketball at 9 p.m.
7 Sally and Robbie / watch a DVD at 9 p.m.
8 Ann / study for an exam at 9 p.m.

10 Write questions in the past continuous. Use the verbs in the box.

~~correct~~ run watch play listen to
do wear have talk to

my teacher / exams last night?
Was my teacher correcting exams last night?
1 your mum / a tracksuit yesterday?
2 Where / they / football yesterday?
3 Who / you / on the telephone?
4 your parents / lunch at home?
5 your brother / in the park last night?
6 When / Louise / her homework?
7 Which TV programme / we / yesterday afternoon?
8 What / you / on your MP3 player?

11 Put the verbs in the correct past simple or past continuous forms.

1 I … (meet) my cousins while I … (visit) Rome.
2 We … (walk) in the park when it … (start) to rain.
3 The teacher … (ask) me a question while I …
(talk) to a friend.
4 We … (lose) the ball while we were … (play)
football.
5 We … (sit) in the café when someone … (take)
our bags.
6 I … (do) my homework when the phone … (ring).

Consolidation

1 Complete the text. Put the verbs in the correct past simple or past continuous forms.

My terrible day

We ... (1 start) our exams last week, but the first day ... (2 not go) very well. While I ... (3 cycle) to school I ... (4 drop) my bag! I ... (5 not / look) when a dog ... (6 run) across the road. I ... (7 stop) quickly but my things ... (8 be) all over the street. I ... (9 not lose) any books, but because of the accident I ... (10 arrive) late for my geography exam. The teacher ... (11 not be) very happy, but I ... (12 explain) the situation and he ... (13 understand). Then, while I ... (14 write) my answers, my pen ... (15 break). I ... (16 not have) another one. I ... (17 ask) the teacher for a pen, but while I ... (18 walk) to his desk, I ... (19 fall) over another student's bag. It ... (20 be) the perfect end to the morning!

2 There is a mistake in each sentence. Find the mistakes and correct them.

1 There was a terrible storm last night. We were very frightening.
2 I don't usually drink some water when I have a meal.
3 Her parents were very afraid of her when she passed all her exams.
4 There was a terrible flood. Some people was swimming in the streets!
5 Jon weren't studying last night. He was watching a DVD.
6 Claire helped me a lot so I buyed her some flowers.
7 Went you to school yesterday? I didn't see you in class.
8 I leaved the house at eight o'clock.
9 There is a new fantastic swimming pool in the town centre.
10 We was watching a boring film when you phoned us.

Reading

1 What type of holiday do you like? Where did you go last year?

2 Read the text. Match the holidays in the photos 1–3 with the people. Which holiday activity do you think is the most interesting?

THIS YEAR IS GOING TO BE DIFFERENT

A ...
My uncle and aunt are giving my cousin and me a fantastic holiday this year - two weeks at a soccer camp in London! Hanna and I are football crazy, so it's the perfect holiday! But we're not going to play football all day. We're going to study English in the mornings and we're going to visit all the famous places in London like Buckingham Palace. We can't wait!

Lea

B ...
This year, I'm not behaving well at home and I'm not studying hard at school. My parents think I'm lazy and moody! They're worried, so they're sending me to a brat camp in the mountains this summer. I'm spending six weeks there! I'm going to walk ten kilometres every day with some other teenagers like me. I'm also going to sleep in a tent. I'm not going to see my friends and I'm not going to enjoy it. It's going to be awful!

Rick

C ...
This summer we're going to stay at home. But it isn't going to be boring because my sister Julia is getting married! Lots of friends and family are coming. My grandparents are going to travel all the way from Sydney, in Australia! Julia is going to wear a beautiful white dress. We're going to have a special meal with all the family and friends. I'm so excited!

Victoria

3 Choose the best title for each holiday.

A ...
B ...
C ...

1 My sister's special day.
2 Camping on the beach.
3 Goals, grammar and sightseeing.
4 My Australian grandparents.
5 Football and more football!
6 A bad boy's holiday!

4 Write *L* (Lea), *R* (Rick) or *V* (Victoria) for each space.

1 ... and ... are happy about what they're going to do in the summer.
2 ... is not going to sleep in a bed.
3 ... and ... are going to be away from their families.
4 ... is not going to a different place.
5 ... is going to be a tourist.
6 ... is having a family celebration.

5 Answer the questions.

1 What are Lea and Hanna going to do in the mornings?
2 Why is a soccer camp the best holiday for Lea and Hanna?
3 Which famous places are Lea and Hanna going to visit?
4 Where is Rick going this summer?
5 How long is Rick staying at the brat camp?
6 What is Rick going to do every day?
7 Why isn't Victoria going away on holiday this year?
8 What is Julia going to wear?
9 Where do Victoria and Julia's grandparents live?

Vocabulary Family

6 Look at Victoria's family tree. Complete the sentences.

1 Julia is Victoria's ... .
2 Albert is Julian's ... .
3 Hugo is Albert's ... .
4 Nina is Emma's ... .
5 Hugo is Victoria's ... .
6 ... is Albert's wife.
7 ... is Lynda's father-in-law.
8 ... is Julian's nephew.
9 ... is Hugo's grandmother.
10 ... is Nina's aunt.

7 Complete the table.

Masculine	Feminine
nephew	(1) ...
(2) ...	daughter
father-in-law	(3) ...
(4) ...	aunt
great-grandfather	(5) ...
(6) ...	wife

 WORKBOOK PAGES 51, 54

TALK ABOUT IT

1 How old are your parents, brothers and sisters?
2 Have you got a lot of uncles and aunts?
3 Where do your cousins live?

Grammar

Future forms *going to*

1 Where do you go for end-of-year school trips? Do you know what you're going to do this year?

2 🔘 Match the theme park rides in the box with the photos 1–3. Then read the text.

roller coaster   water flume   ferris wheel

What are you going to do for your end-of-year school trip? Next Wednesday we're going to visit a theme park. The theme park has four different areas. There is the *Wild West*, *Polynesia*, *Future World* and the *Land of the Pharaohs*. In these areas there are different shows, but my class isn't going to see them. What are we going to do? Well, we love the rides and we're going to try all of them. My favourite is the roller coaster, but there is one ride I'm not going to get on: the ferris wheel. I'm frightened of that one, but I'm not going to tell the others!

3 Look at the rule and the example sentences. Can you find other examples of *going to* in the text?

> When we talk about the future we can use *be* + *going to* + infinitive.
> Next week we're going to visit a theme park.
> There is one ride I'm not going to get on.
> What are you going to do for your end-of-year school trip?

4 Write sentences with *going to*.

1 we / eat sandwiches
2 my best friend / buy some souvenirs
3 I / take photographs
4 we / get on the roller coaster
5 we / arrive home late

5 Look back at the text in exercise 2. Then correct the mistakes in the email.

From Tim@highscore.com
Date Tuesday, 15ᵗʰ June
To   Simon@highscore.com

Dear Simon

How are you? I'm very excited about our end-of-year school trip!

~~We're going to visit a castle.~~

We're going to stay for two days. The class is going to watch all the shows. I'm going to try the ferris wheel.

I'm going to tell the others.

Bye!

Tim

6 Write questions for the answers.

1 What / you / eat?
   We're going to eat fast food.
2 Which ride / you / try?
   I'm going to try the water flume.
3 You / see a show?
   Yes, we're going to see a show.
4 When / you / arrive home?
   We're going to arrive home very late.
5 You / buy any souvenirs?
   Yes, I'm going to buy some souvenirs.

7 Match the future time expressions 1–8 with the dates and times a–h.

Today is Monday 4th April.

1 My aunt from Wales is going to visit us next week.
2 We're going to watch a play in two months' time.
3 I'm going to work harder this month.
4 We're going to catch a plane tomorrow morning.
5 We're going to visit our grandparents next weekend.
6 I'm going to study French in the next school year.
7 We're going to play basketball tomorrow afternoon.
8 I'm going to do my homework this evening.

a 11th April
b April
c September
d 4th April, 7 p.m.
e 5th April, 5 p.m.
f 9th and 10th April
g 5th April, 9 a.m.
h June

Consolidation

8 Complete the dialogue with the correct form of *going to* and the verbs in brackets. Where there is no verb, use a future time expression from the box.

tonight   tomorrow morning
in three months' time   next weekend

Hassan	Where … **(1 you / spend)** the summer?
Samir	Well, this year I … **(2 study)** English in the USA.
Hassan	Fantastic! Who … **(3 you / stay)** with?
Samir	With my dad's friends. I'm meeting them **(4)** …, on Saturday. They're arriving on Friday, but they … **(5 not / have)** a holiday. They're coming to work here in Jordan for three months. Then **(6)** … , in July, I … **(7 travel)** to New York with them.
Hassan	… **(8 you / study)** in New York?
Samir	Yes, but I … **(9 not / stay)** in New York. I'm staying in Rochester.
Hassan	Rochester?
Samir	Yes, it's a small town near New York. I … **(10 find)** it on the internet **(11)** … , after school.
Hassan	Well, you can tell me about it **(12)** … before our English class.

Future forms Present continuous

9 Look at the rules and the sentences.

> There is often no difference between the present continuous for the future and *going to*. We also use the same future time expressions.
>
> *Next week we're going to visit a theme park.*
> *Next week we're visiting a theme park.*
>
> *There is one ride I'm not going to get on.*
> *There is one ride I'm not getting on.*
>
> *What are you going to do for your end-of-year school trip?*
> *What are you doing for your end-of-year school trip?*

Quick tip We usually use the present continuous with the verbs *come* and *go* when we talk about the future: *My grandparents are coming from Sydney next week. I'm not going to the beach this summer.*

10 Complete the sentences in the present continuous about the school trip.

> SCHOOL TRIP TO THEME PARK
> • meet at school next Thursday at 7.30 a.m.
> • the coach leaves at 8 a.m.
> • have lunch at 1 p.m.
> • return to the coach at 7 p.m.
> • arrive at school at 11 p.m.

1 We … .
2 The coach … .
3 We … .
4 We … .
5 We … .

GRAMMAR REFERENCE PAGE 107
WORKBOOK PAGE 52

Communication

Vocabulary *go, make, do* and *have*

1 Do you go to a camp in the summer? Which activities do you think you can do at a summer camp?

2 Match the words in the box with the correct verbs.

a meal   homework   on foot   a good time
a mistake   a shower   a picnic   the bed
on a day trip   the washing up   friends
a barbecue

| go | make | do | have |

Listening Summer camp

3 Listen and answer the questions.

1 Which water activities does Dale talk about?
2 Which mountain activity does Dale talk about?
3 What do they do in the evenings?
4 How do the children travel on the day trips?
5 What time do they get up?
6 What do they do before breakfast?
7 When is the camp starting?
8 Does Virginia want to go to the camp?

Speaking Plans for next summer

4 In pairs, read the dialogue.

A What are you going to do next summer?
B I'm going to study English in San Francisco.
A That's great! Who are you going with?
B I'm going with my cousins. What are you going to do?
A Well, I'm going to …

5 Make up a dialogue about next summer. Act out your dialogue in class.

➡ WORKBOOK PAGE 54

Culture focus

1 🔘 Read the text. Match the photos 1–3 with the festivals in the text.

Holidays American style!

The Fourth of July

The Fourth of July is the coolest holiday of the year. In the morning we always go downtown to watch the parade, and this year my school is walking in it. Best of all, my brother is carrying the flag. My parents are going to be really proud of him! Then in the afternoon we always have a picnic. This year we're going to have a big school picnic by the Potomac river. All the mums, dads and grandparents are coming too. Finally, in the evening, we always watch a really fantastic firework display. Why do we celebrate the Fourth of July? It's the day in 1776 when we became independent from the British – a very important date for us!

Thanksgiving day

In the USA, on the fourth Thursday of every November we celebrate Thanksgiving day with our families. We now live in Washington, but we're going to drive back to Chicago to be with our grandparents. Most Americans travel to spend this day at home with their families. The most important part of the day is the big family dinner and the most popular meal is turkey. What are we celebrating? Well, traditionally it's a day to give thanks for all the food collected on the farms for the winter. Today, we have all the food we need, but Thanksgiving day is the most popular family day in the USA.

2 Mark the sentences *FJ* (the Fourth of July), *TD* (Thanksgiving day) or *B* (Both).

1 People travel for the celebration.
2 People celebrate with their families.
3 People celebrate something that happened a long time ago.
4 People celebrate at home.
5 Food is part of the celebration.
6 There is more than one activity in the celebrations.

3 Answer the questions.

1 Which three things do Americans do on the Fourth of July?
2 What is the boy's brother going to do on the Fourth of July?
3 Who is going to the school picnic?
4 Where do most Americans spend Thanksgiving day?
5 What do most Americans eat on Thanksgiving day?
6 Why do Americans celebrate Thanksgiving day?

TALK ABOUT IT

1 Do you have a special festival in your country?
2 What do you do? What activities do they organise in your town? Are there special things for children and young people?

Writing

An informal letter
Parts of a letter

① Read Janette's letter and look at the photos. Which holiday did she go on last year? Which holiday is she going on this year?

② Match the phrases in the box with the spaces 1–6 in the letter.

Best wishes   35, rue du Mont,
Write to me soon   Dear Bernice   6th April
75889 Paris

(1) ...

(2) ...

(3) ...

(4) ... ,

   How are you? I hope you and your family are well. I had a great time with you in London last year and I learnt a lot of English. I've got an English exam next week, so I hope I'm going to pass!
   This summer we're doing something very different. We're going to South Africa! We're going on safari and at night we're going to make camp fires and sleep in tents. My brother is worried that a lion is going to eat us when we're sleeping, but my parents said it's very safe. I can't wait!
   Anyway, what are you going to do this summer? Are you coming to France to study French?

   (5) ... !

   (6) ... ,

   Janette

③ Read the letter and choose the correct answer.

When you write an informal letter ...

1   write / **don't write** your name with your address.
2   write the date **after** / **before** the address.
3   ask / **don't ask** your friend questions.
4   finish / **don't finish** the letter with your name and surname.

④ You are going to write a letter to a friend. First plan your three main paragraphs:

*   Ask your friend how he / she is. Ask about his / her family. What are you doing at the moment?
*   What are you going to do in the summer?
*   Ask your friend what he / she is going to do in the summer.

⑤ Write your letter. Remember that:

*   you need to include your address and the date.
*   you need to check for punctuation and vocabulary mistakes.
*   you can use both the *going to* and the present continuous for the future.

 WORKBOOK PAGE 55

72   UNIT 7

Quick check

Vocabulary

1 Complete the sentences.

1 Your sister is your mother's ....
2 Your mother's father is your ....
3 Your dad's brother's son is your ....
4 Your sister's daughter is your ....
5 Your father's sister is your ....
6 Your mother is your father's ....

2 Choose the answer that is wrong.

1 Go …
   a on a day trip   b homework   c on foot
2 Make …
   a homework   b friends   c the bed
3 Have …
   a a good time   b dinner   c a day trip
4 Do …
   a a shower   b sport   c homework
5 Make …
   a your bed   b the washing up   c a mistake
6 Have …
   a a barbeque   b a picnic   c sport

Vocabulary review: Units 1–7

3 Choose the correct answer for each space.

1 The plane is going to … at 5 p.m.
2 My mum is … of flying.
3 We are going to … at 3 p.m.
4 I'm going to buy a book from the ....
5 I'm … that we're going to miss the flight.

1 a take off   b get off
2 a frightening   b frightened
3 a check in   b catch
4 a bookshop   b library
5 a worried   b glad

Grammar

4 Write affirmative or negative sentences or questions with the correct form of *going to*. Use the verbs in the box.

make   have   take   do   get on   travel   study

Simon / the washing up?
Is Simon going to do the washing up?

1 They / lunch ✓
2 we / by plane ?
3 she / a new friend ?
4 We / the roller coaster ✗
5 He / photos ✓
6 I / English in Ireland ✗

5 Put the time expressions a–j in order from 1–10.

e this afternoon

a next weekend   f tomorrow afternoon
b tomorrow morning   g in six months' time
c next year   h this evening
d next month   i tomorrow evening
e this afternoon   j in two years' time

6 Complete the sentences and questions in the present continuous form of the verbs in brackets.

1 We … (come) to stay with you next week.
2 … (he / go) on holiday in June?
3 We … (eat) chicken tonight.
4 They … (not / play) tennis tomorrow.
5 … (they / have) a meeting on Saturday?
6 I … (do) my homework at 7 p.m.

Grammar review: Units 1–7

7 There are mistakes in five of the sentences. Find the mistakes and correct them.

1 We was studying in class when the storm started.
2 The plane didn't takes off at 10 p.m.
3 They haven't got some magazines.
4 I always do my homework before I have dinner.
5 Argentina is hottest than England.
6 What they were wearing at the party?

Reading

1 Which things in the photos are bad for the planet?

2 💿 Read the text. Which of your answers from exercise 1 are in the text?

Be green: help your planet!

1 Did you know you can help protect the planet? Don't waste the things you don't want by throwing them away! Local 'green' companies can make those old posters and magazines into recycled paper, and they can transform your old mobile phone into a new one. You and your family can help too. Collect those t–shirts and jeans that are too small for you and give them to a charity.

2 Of course, most people need a break at school or work. But if you drink from plastic bottles, you won't help the planet. It looks harmless, but plastic is a material that is difficult to recycle. And if you eat a snack, make sure it comes in just one bag or box. A lot of modern food products have lots of packaging and it's a waste! Why not drink fruit juice from a glass bottle and make a sandwich? Glass is easy to recycle and a homemade sandwich is better for you and for the environment!

3 When you go shopping, think before you buy! Are your trainers really old? Do you really need a new MP3 player? Remember, we don't need to use the world's resources to look cool. If you only buy the things that are really necessary, you'll help save the planet and your money!

4 What else can you do? Don't have a bath, have a shower! If you have a shower, you'll use less water. When you have a bath you use approximately 90 litres of water, but only 30 litres when you have a shower. And don't leave the tap on when you brush your teeth! Water is one of our most important natural resources, and you can help save it.

5 Will our planet survive? Well, if we all help, it will have a better chance. Why don't you start saving the planet at home this evening?

3 Choose the correct answer.

1 Local green companies …
   a sell posters, magazines and
     mobile phones.
   b work with old paper and
     mobile phones.
2 Plastic bottles are …
   a bad for the environment.
   b good for the environment.
3 A lot of food products come in …
   a lots of bags and boxes.
   b only one bag or box.
4 If you have a bath, you'll …
   a save water.
   b waste water.
5 Don't …
   a brush your teeth.
   b leave the tap on.
6 The planet will survive if …
   a we stay at home this evening.
   b everybody helps.

4 Are these sentences true or false? Explain your answers.

1 There are companies that reuse old
  things.
2 They use plastic and glass to make
  bottles.
3 Modern food products are a waste.
4 You use more water in a bath than
  in a shower.
5 Water is the most important natural
  resource in the world.

5 Match the topics a–e with the paragraphs 1–5.

a the bathroom
b money and resources
c things you've got at home
d the planet's future
e things you buy at a supermarket

6 Find six things in the text that we can do to help the planet.

Vocabulary Environment

7 Match the words in the box with the photos 1–5.

packaging   recycle   bottle bank   pollution   throw away

8 Choose the correct answer.

1 When you have a bath you **damage** / **waste** water.
2 When you travel by car you **damage** / **waste** the environment.

9 Find the opposites of *damage* and *waste* in the text.

10 Match the words in the box with the definitions 1–3.

environment   conservation   green

1 The natural world where people, plants and animals live.
2 Stopping the destruction of plants, animals and the planet.
3 This is what you are if you are friendly to the natural world.

11 Do the quiz. How green are you? Then listen. How many points have you got?

Are you green? Do you want to help our planet? Do this week's exciting quiz and find out!
1 Is plastic difficult to recycle?
2 Plastic bottles are better for the environment than glass bottles. True or false?
3 Do you throw away your old things and not recycle them?
4 Do you eat snacks that have a lot of packaging e.g. paper, boxes or bags?
5 Do you help to clean pollution from beaches or rivers?

WORKBOOK PAGES 57, 60

TALK ABOUT IT

Think of three things to make our homes and schools greener. Discuss your ideas with your partner.

Future forms *will*

1 Read the advert. Why are tigers in danger?

SAVE THE WORLD'S TIGERS

In 1906 there were 100,000 tigers in the world. Today there are only 6,000! If more tigers die, they'll disappear from our planet. Send us some money now!

Will the situation improve? Only with your help! Don't wait! Soon, it'll be too late!

What are we going to do with your money?

We're going to build a tiger reservation in India to protect the tigers. There will be food on the reservation for the tigers, so they won't enter villages looking for food. Village people often kill tigers because they are frightened of them.

The world is changing and tigers won't survive in the modern world. Send us your name and address or your email address and we'll send you our information pack.

Email: help@savetigers.com

phone: 01632 707070

2 Look at the rules and the sentences.

> When we make predictions about the future we use *will / won't* + infinitive.
> *Soon, it'll be too late!*
> *Tigers won't survive in the modern world.*
> *Will the situation improve?*

3 Complete the sentences with *will / won't* and the verbs in the box.

> pass rain disappear recycle win go
> do be

1 A German football team … the Champions League next year. ✓
2 I didn't do my homework. The teacher … happy. ✗
3 A green company … my old school books. ✓
4 Lots of animals … from the planet by 2020. ✓
5 We … camping this weekend. ✗
6 I … any work in the school holidays. ✗
7 We … our exams next month. ✓
8 It … tomorrow. ✓

4 Order the words to make questions.

1 will / When / you / arrive?
2 the game? / Who / win / will
3 the weather / good? / be / Will
4 take off / the plane / at 10 a.m.?/ Will
5 meet? / they / will / Where
6 on holiday? / Will / make friends / we
7 Will / this winter? / snow / it
8 film / enjoy? / they / will / Which

> **Quick tip** We often use *think* or *probably* when we make predictions.
> *I think Betis will win the league next year.*
> *She thinks people will live on planet Mars one day.*
> *Maria will probably go to university when she's eighteen.*

5 Write six sentences about the things you think you will do this summer, next school year and when you're eighteen.

I think I'll visit my friend in Oxford this summer.

First conditional

6 Look at the rule and the example sentences.

> When we want to talk about a possible future situation we use the first conditional:
> *if* + present simple + *will*.
> *If you have a shower, you'll use less water.*
> **or**
> *will* + *if* + present simple
> *You'll use less water if you have a shower.*

> **Quick tip** When we start the sentence with *if*, we use a comma after the present simple.
> *If more tigers die, they'll disappear from our planet.*

7 Match 1–6 with a–f to make sentences.

1 If we study hard,	a the play will be good.
2 If I've got homework,	b she won't play in the school orchestra.
3 If my sister goes to London,	c there will be a drought.
4 If we rehearse a lot,	d we'll pass our exams.
5 If it doesn't rain,	e I'll do it before dinner.
6 If she doesn't practise the violin,	f she'll learn a lot of English.

8 Complete the sentences with the correct forms of the verbs in brackets.

1 If you … (send) us some money, we … (build) a tiger reservation.
2 We … (give) food to the tigers if we … (build) a tiger reservation.
3 If we … (give) food to the tigers, they … (not enter) the villages.
4 The people … (be) happy if the tigers … (not enter) the villages.
5 If the people … (be) happy, the Indian tigers … (survive).
6 If the Indian tigers … (survive), other animals … (have) hope.

Consolidation

9 Complete the text with the correct form of the verbs in brackets. Then listen and check.

About 25,000 square kilometres of the Amazon rainforest disappear every year. If this … (**1** continue), the world … (**2** have) problems. What problems … the world … (**3** have)? Scientists say there … (**4** be) fewer animals and plants. 30% of all plants and animals live in the rainforest. We use a lot of the plants to make new medicines so we … (**5** not have) new medicines if we … (**6** destroy) the plants. If the rainforest … (**7** become) smaller, it … (**8** not rain) a lot in some parts of Brazil and there … (**9** be) floods in other places. … the entire rainforest … (**10** disappear)? It … (**11** not disappear) tomorrow, but we must protect it. The rainforest is a very special place on our planet.

The imperative

10 Look at the rules and the example sentences.

When we want to tell people what to do we use the imperative.
For the affirmative form we use the infinitive: *Send us some money now!*
For the negative form we use *don't* + infinitive: *Don't wait for me!*

11 Make affirmative or negative imperatives with a word or phrase from each box.

~~be~~   smoke
wait   eat

cigarettes
for me   ~~quiet~~
all your dinner

Be quiet!

  GRAMMAR REFERENCE PAGE 108
WORKBOOK PAGE 58

Communication

Vocabulary Campaigns

1 Match the phrases in the box with the pictures 1–7.

> have a meeting   wear wristbands
> sign a petition   collect money   write letters
> go on a demonstration   put up posters

Listening Save the park!

2 🔘 **Which things do Nick, Lesley and Elaine mention? Listen and tick ✓.**

a petition ☐   wristbands ☐

a meeting ☐   posters ☐

money ☐   a demonstration ☐

letters ☐

3 🔘 **Listen again and complete the sentences with the words in the box.**

> their friends and families   the young children
> the town hall   the mums and dads   the school
> school students

1 The people that go to the park are …, …, and ….
2 The meetings are for … and ….
3 The posters are for ….
4 They are going to send a letter to ….
5 The people that will sign the petition are …, …, and ….
6 They will send the petition to ….

Speaking Environment

4 🔘 **In pairs, read the dialogue.**

> **A** Are you green? What do you and your family do to help the environment?
> **B** Yes, we're quite green - we always recycle bottles.
> **A** Do you do anything else?
> **B** I wear a wristband. And last week my brother went on a demonstration!

5 **Are you interested in the environment? Make up a dialogue about what you do. Act out your dialogue in class.**

➡ **WORKBOOK PAGE 60**

Culture focus

1 🔊 **Listen. Which animals can you hear?**

2 🔊 **Read the text. How does Utete's father know where the animals are?**

Etosha National Park · Otjinene · Windhoek · Botswana · Namibia · Kalahari Desert · South Africa

ON SAFARI

My name's Utete and I live in Otjinene. Otjinene is a village in the Kalahari Desert in eastern Namibia. We moved to northern Namibia six years ago because my dad started a new job at the Etosha National Park. My dad is a guide for the tourists. When I'm not at school I sometimes go on safari with him. I love it! He knows everything about the animals and their environment and I learn a lot from him.

My dad always knows where the animals are. He recognises the different sounds they make. When he looks at the ground he can say which animals are near, and how many there are. The plants and trees also show my dad which animals are near us, because he knows which plants the animals like eating. The tourists are always astonished!

Thanks to going on safari with my dad, I think I'll study zoology in the future. We need people to learn how to protect our animals and our natural resources. Animals like lions, elephants and rhinoceros are important in our culture. If we lose these animals, we'll lose our traditions too. The animals are also important because tourists come to see them. But there are people that come to kill the animals. If we can't stop them, we won't have any safaris in the future and the world will be a sadder place.

3 **Answer the questions.**

1 Where does Utete's father work?
2 What does Utete sometimes do when she's not at school?
3 What is Utete's plan for the future?
4 What do they need people to do?
5 Which animals are important in Namibian culture?
6 What will happen if they can't stop the people that kill animals?

TALK ABOUT IT

1 Do you like animals?
2 What are your favourite animals? Why?

Writing

A poster Subject pronouns

1 Match the subject pronouns 1–8 in the poster with the phrases in the box.

> the director of *Friends Of The Sea*   the beach   the person reading the poster   the mayor
> the posters   the demonstration   Parker Road School   a group of students

PARKER ROAD SCHOOL STUDENTS SAY SAVE OUR BEACH!

Our local government says it doesn't have any money to clean the beach! If (**1**) <u>we</u> don't do something, (**2**) <u>it</u> won't be clean for the summer. What are we going to do? Next Saturday we're going to organise a demonstration. (**3**) <u>It</u> is going to be in the town centre. The director of the green organisation *Friends Of The Sea* is coming, and (**4**) <u>she</u>'s going to

explain the situation. We'll also start a petition and a group of students will take it to the town hall. (**5**) <u>They</u>'re also going to ask the mayor for more rubbish bins on the beach and a new volleyball area. What can (**6**) *you* do? **Come to our meeting on Monday 25th May in room 8.**

There is lots of work to do! We need lots of new posters. (**7**) <u>They</u> will tell everybody about the demonstration and when it is going to happen. We also need people to write and send letters and emails to the mayor. (**8**) <u>He</u> doesn't know how important the beach is for the people of the town!

COME AND HELP MAKE OUR BEACH BEAUTIFUL AGAIN!

2 You are going to make a poster. First think about these questions:

- What do you want to tell people about? (animals in danger / something that is happening in your town)
- What will happen if people don't help with the problem?
- What will your organisation do?
- What can people do to help your organisation?
- What meetings or demonstrations are you going to have?
- When and where will they be?

3 Think about the presentation of your poster.

- Will it have any photos?
- Will you write in different colours so that people notice it?

4 Make your poster. Remember to:

- use subject pronouns when you can (don't repeat names).
- check that there are no punctuation or vocabulary mistakes.
- use *will*, the first conditional and imperatives correctly.

 **WORKBOOK PAGE 61**

Quick check

Vocabulary

1 Choose the correct answer.

1 People that look after the … are green.
   a environment   b packaging
2 Don't throw things away. … them!
   a Damage   b Recycle
3 What's the opposite of *waste*?
   a save   b throw away
4 What's the opposite of *damage*?
   a protect   b recycle
5 Which material do you put in a bottle bank?
   a plastic   b glass
6 Bags and boxes are examples of …
   a pollution   b packaging.
7 Conservation helps …
   a packaging   b the environment.
8 … bottles are better for drinks because they are easier to recycle.
   a Glass   b Plastic

2 Complete the sentences with the verbs in the box.

> have   go on   sign   put up   collect
> write   wear

1 The first wristbands were against cancer. Now people … wristbands to help lots of organisations.
2 We're going to … money for *Tigers in danger*.
3 If we … the demonstration, the town hall will clean the beach.
4 We're going to do more than … letters. We're going to … a meeting. Then we can ask everybody to … a petition.
5 I'm going to … a poster about the meeting.

Vocabulary review: Units 1–8

3 Which word is not correct in each group?

1 a shower   a barbeque   homework   a picnic
2 enthusiastic   glad   upset   proud
3 son   niece   sister   daughter
4 interesting   frightened   surprising   fascinating
5 nephew   dad   husband   aunt
6 mistakes   friends   your bed   an exam

Grammar

4 Complete the sentences with the affirmative or negative imperative form of the verbs in the box.

> use   listen   eat   arrive   talk   smoke

1 … in the no-smoking zone!
2 … all your vegetables!
3 … your mobile phones in the exam!
4 … at school on time!
5 … to your teachers!
6 … in the library!

5 Write affirmative or negative sentences or questions with *will* / *won't*. Use the verbs in the box.

> save   make   sign   go on   recycle   have

1 They / a demonstration ✗
2 David / his old magazines ?
3 they / their beds ?
4 I / a good time on holiday ✓
5 We / water with a swimming pool ✗
6 Sarah / the petition ✓

6 Make first conditional sentences.

1 we / If / we'll / visit the Statue of Liberty. / go to New York,
2 be late / You'll / you / if / don't get up.
3 buy you a present. / If / pass the exams, / I'll / you
4 arrives late, / miss the plane. / she / she'll / If
5 stay at home / if / it / They'll / rains.
6 we / have a celebration. / we'll / If / win the match,

Grammar review: Units 1–8

7 Complete the sentences with the words in the box.

> some   afternoon   wasn't   were   any   did

1 … you sleeping at twelve o'clock?
2 They've got … new CDs.
3 We're going to play volleyball tomorrow … .
4 … they have a barbecue?
5 He … doing his homework.
6 Have you got … fruit?

9 | Changes

Reading

1 How has your life changed in recent years? Have you changed school, home or city? Do you think you have changed?

2 Read the text. Does the text mention any of the changes you discussed in exercise 1?

HOW I'VE CHANGED

1 Lots of things have changed in my life in recent years. Firstly, I've changed school. It was difficult at first, but now I enjoy it. My classmates are great, **A** ... . Well, there is one boy I don't like, because he is sometimes a bully to a friend of ours, but we protect her.

2 Another difference in the last two or three years has been in my school work. There's more of it, **B** ... ! I've got lots of new subjects and more text books. I've also got two exercise books for each subject: **C** ... . I've got a locker at school, but I take lots of books home. I don't need a rucksack, I need a supermarket trolley!

3 I've changed the way I look too. I still like wearing jeans and t-shirts but now I also like wearing different clothes when I go out with my friends. I've started wearing skirts and lots of jewellery. My mum helps me get ready before I go out. We have good fun, **D** ... ! I've also changed my hairstyle. It's longer **E** ... !

4 Now I also do different things in my spare time. I like spending more time with my friends. We meet in town on Saturdays and we spend our pocket money at the shops or the cinema. I also spend more time in my bedroom. I've put up some new posters **F** ... , but my mum says my bedroom is the only thing that hasn't changed. It has always been very untidy!

3 The writer is a girl. How do we know?

4 Choose the best title for the text.

1 Who am I?
2 My best friend is my mum
3 Changing with the years
4 School is different

5 Match the information 1–6 with the spaces A–F.

1 one for class work and one for homework
2 and I sometimes change the colour
3 and I've made lots of friends
4 but she doesn't always like the way I dress
5 and I've moved the furniture
6 especially homework and exams

6 Which paragraph …

a tells us about the writer's weekend activities?
b tells us about what the writer wears?
c tells us about the writer's school materials?
d tells us about a problem at school?

7 Are the sentences true or false? Explain your answers.

1 The writer now likes her school.
2 She didn't like school at first.
3 Her friends sometimes protect her.
4 She's got two text books for each subject.
5 She leaves all her books at school.
6 She doesn't always dress in jeans and t-shirts.
7 She goes shopping with her friends at the weekends.
8 Her mum thinks her bedroom is tidy.

Vocabulary School

8 Match the words in the box with the pictures 1–5.

text book   exercise book   locker   rucksack   desk

9 Match the words 1–6 with the definitions a–f.

1 A bully is …
2 A subject is …
3 A lesson is …
4 Homework is …
5 An exam is …
6 Rules are …

a the things we can or can't do at school and at home.
b a thing like English, maths, biology etc. that you study at school.
c a test of what you know about something.
d a period of time when you study a subject in class with your teacher.
e a student that frightens other students.
f the work that teachers ask students to do at home.

 **WORKBOOK PAGES 63, 66**

TALK ABOUT IT

1 Which subjects do you get the most homework for?
2 When do you do your homework?
3 How much spare time do you have in the evening?
4 Are there any rules at home or at school that you don't like?

Grammar

Present perfect Introduction

1 🔘 **Read and match the text with one of the pictures 1–2. What are the differences between the pictures?**

Have your parents ever painted your bedroom? Have you asked them if you can paint it? They'll be happy if you do the work! I've painted my room in Arsenal's colours. My parents say they've never seen a red and white bedroom! I've also put up some *Star Wars* and Arsenal posters. I haven't painted the furniture but I've put my desk next to the window. There's a computer on my desk, but I haven't got a TV. I've never watched TV in my room because it's against the rules at home! Well, do you want a cool bedroom? My sister hasn't painted hers before, but now she's going to do it. What are you waiting for?

2 **Look at the rules and the example sentences.**

> To make the present perfect, we use *has / have* or *hasn't / haven't* + past participle.
> *I've painted my room in Arsenal's colours.*
> *I haven't painted the furniture...*
> *Have you asked them if you can paint it?*

3 **Tick ✓ the present perfect sentences.**

1 I've also put up some *Star Wars* posters.
2 I haven't got a TV.
3 Lots of things have changed in my life in recent years.

4 **Look at the rule and complete the table.**

> Regular past participles end in *-ed*.
> Irregular past participles are all different.

Quick tip Turn to page 119 for a list of irregular past participles. Try to learn a few every day!

Infinitive	Past participle
look	(1)…
(2)…	walked
have	(3)…
(4)…	eaten
speak	(5)…

5 **Complete the sentences using the present perfect form of the verbs in the box.**

> do   win   cycle
> swim   run   climb

This year …
1 Stan … in the New York marathon.
2 He … the Everest and K2 mountains.
3 He … from England to France.
4 He … two Olympic medals.
5 He … in the Tour de France.
6 Stan … a lot of things!

6 Look back at exercise 5. Correct the mistakes in the newspaper report.

> Stan Storey from London has had a fantastic year. ~~Stan has sailed from England to France~~ and he's won five Olympic medals. He's also walked in the New York marathon and he's climbed Mont Blanc. Stan has also watched the Tour de France.
>
> *Stan hasn't sailed from England to France. He's swum from England to France.*

7 Write questions for the answers.

Have you been on holiday this year?
No, I haven't been on holiday this year.

1 Yes, my sister has started university.
2 No, my parents haven't bought a new car.
3 Yes, I have seen my cousins this week.
4 Yes, we have played basketball this term.
5 Yes, my brother has had a good year at school.
6 Yes, I've changed a lot this year.

Present perfect *ever* and *never*

8 Look at the rules and the example sentences.

> **We often use *ever* in present perfect questions to say 'at any time in your life'.**
> ***Have your parents ever painted your bedroom?***
>
> **We often use *never* in present perfect sentences to say 'at no time in your life'.**
> ***They've never seen a red and white bedroom!***

9 Write sentences with *never* or questions with *ever*.

1 You / eat / Indian food ?
2 My grandparents / visit / London. ✗
3 My dad / use / an MP3 player. ✗
4 They / study / Japanese ?
5 Your sister / paint / her bedroom ?
6 I / drink / coffee. ✗

Consolidation

10 Complete the text with the correct present perfect form of the verbs in brackets. Then listen and check.

… you … (1 ever / want) to change your life and do something different? Well, that's what the Bourton family … (2 do). They … (3 visit) four continents and they … (4 explore) 25 countries in the last six years and they haven't finished! They … (5 spend) five years on a eleven metre boat. Mum, Sue, is a teacher and she … (6 teach) her children, Jane and Mike, everything they know. They … (7 never / go) to school! 'We … (8 make) lots of friends around the world,' says Mike. They … (9 not / stay) in one place for more than two months and now they're sailing to New Zealand.

➡ GRAMMAR REFERENCE PAGE 109
WORKBOOK PAGE 64

Communication

Vocabulary In the country

1 Match the words in the box with the numbers 1–9.

woods   farm   hill   cottage   stream   field   valley   footpath   village

Listening Changes in a town

2 💿 You are going to hear a student asking a woman about the town of Brinklow. Listen and tick ✓ the places that she mentions.

car park	☐	factory	☐
musuem	☐	park	☐
woods	☐	cinema	☐
book shop	☐	footpath	☐
hospital	☐	village	☐
cottages	☐	hill	☐
stream	☐	library	☐
farm	☐	field	☐

3 💿 Listen again and complete the lists.

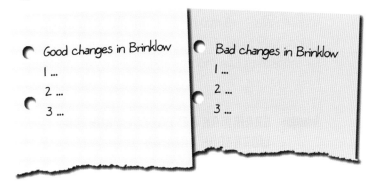

Good changes in Brinklow
1 ...
2 ...
3 ...

Bad changes in Brinklow
1 ...
2 ...
3 ...

Speaking In your town

4 💿 In pairs, read the dialogue.

> **A** What changes have happened in our town?
> **B** Well, the old cinema has become a big multiplex cinema.
> **A** Yes, and now there's a big sports centre. I think it's great.
> **B** But there have been some bad changes, too.
> **A** Yes. I don't like the …

5 Make up a dialogue about the changes in your town. Act out your dialogue in class.

WORKBOOK PAGE 66

Culture focus

1 In pairs, do the quiz.

USA Schools Quiz

1 A secondary school is called … in the USA.
   a an elementary school b a high school.
2 In the USA they call school years … .
   a grades b levels.
3 They call football a different name in the USA. It is … .
   a softball b soccer
4 The school summer holidays in the USA are … in your country.
   a the same as b shorter than
5 The school day in the USA is … than in your country.
   a longer than b shorter than

2 Look at the photos and read the title of the text. What do you think it is about?

3 Read the text. What differences can you find between American school life and school life in your country?

MOVING HOME

I'm from Tokyo but now we live in San Francisco, California. A lot of my family live here so we came to San Francisco to be closer to them. Of course, I know that the family is important, but at first it was very difficult. I didn't like leaving all my friends at my old school in Tokyo.

Now, after a year in ninth grade, I've made lots of new friends here at Palmers Park High School, San Francisco. But I've had some surprises. On my first day at school there were security men at the school doors. They were looking for guns! That was very frightening!

Another surprise was the school timetable. We begin classes at 8 a.m. and finish at 3.15 p.m. Lunch is from midday until 1 p.m.! If you want to eat fast food, an American school is the place for you! You can eat hamburgers, pizza and hotdogs every day. There are also lots of machines in the school that sell chocolate, sweets and cola. All the students do sports after school, and they need to!

Now I'm more positive about San Francisco. I've learnt a lot of English. I've got two cultures now, and that's great. I'm also going to learn to drive soon. You can learn to drive when you're fifteen in California. All the eleventh grade students come to school in their cars! But the best thing about the USA is the people because they are really friendly.

4 Answer the questions.

1 What didn't the writer like about leaving Tokyo?
2 What has the writer made at Palmers Park School?
3 What were the security men searching for?
4 What can you eat for lunch at an American school?
5 What other things can students eat and drink at an American school?
6 Why do the students need to do sport?
7 How does the writer feel about living in San Francisco now? Why?
8 What is the writer going to learn soon?

TALK ABOUT IT

1 Have you ever changed home, school, town or country? Why?
2 Do you think you will change home, school, town or country in the future? Why?

Writing

A magazine interview
Checking your work

1 Match the questions a–d with the answers 1–4. (Don't worry about the mistakes in the text.)

a Have you made a new record?
b And finally, have you ever made a film?
c Firstly, have you had a good year?
d Has your life changed in other ways?

Your favourite magazine, *Meet the Stars*, has interviewed Britain's new number one pop star, Michelle McMichaels.

(1) No, not good – it've been fantastic! I've become a star and my life has changed completely? People stop I in the street. I'm famous! It's wonderful.

(2) Yes, I've buyed a beautiful old car park in a small village near Edinburgh. I go there to relax in my spare life after concerts.

(3) No I havent. I've done lots of concerts this year, but I'm going to make a new CD next summer. It was going to be great!

(4) No, I've never made one, but my agent is talking with a Hollywood studio. so who knows? Am I going to win an Oscar next year.

If you'll read *Meet the Stars*, you'll see if Michelle is lucky in Hollywood!

2 Read the interview again and find ten mistakes. There are grammar, vocabulary and punctuation mistakes.

3 Use this table to organise and correct the mistakes.

Type of mistake	Mistake	Correction
Grammar	*it've been fantastic!*	*it's been fantastic!*

4 You are going to write an interview with a famous person. First prepare the magazine reporter's questions.

- Ask him / her what he / she has done this year.
- Ask him / her if fame has changed his / her life.
- What other things do you want to know?

5 Now invent the famous person's answers.

6 Write the interview. Remember to:

- write an introduction and a finishing sentence for your interview.
- think about the presentation of your interview.
- check that there are no grammar, punctuation or vocabulary mistakes.
- use the present perfect correctly in your interview.

 WORKBOOK PAGE 67

Quick check

Vocabulary

1 **Choose the correct answer.**

1 A book you write in at school.
   a an exercise book   b a text book
2 A place to leave your books at school.
   a a rucksack   b a locker
3 Something a teacher gives you to do after school.
   a an exam   b homework
4 History and physics are examples of ...
   a rules   b subjects
5 You sit at this table when you study.
   a a desk   b bed
6 A test on the things you've studied.
   a an exam   b a subject

2 **Match the words in the box with the definitions 1–6.**

footpath   cottage   stream   field   farm   hill

1 A small river.
2 A green place in the country where animals eat.
3 A small country house.
4 A house and buildings in the country where people look after animals and grow crops.
5 It isn't as big as a mountain.
6 You walk on this in the countryside.

Vocabulary review: Units 1–9

3 **Choose the correct answer.**

My city has changed a lot and I don't like it. All the new
(1) ... they've built are horrible. Last week I went on a
(2) ... to show I'm not happy with what has happened.
We want a city that helps the (3) ..., not one that is full
of cars and (4) ... . I like going to school on (5) ... but
with the busy new (6) ... it's very difficult.

1 a car parks   b farms
2 a wristband   b demonstration
3 a environment   b packaging
4 a recycling   b pollution
5 a foot   b train
6 a footpath   b road

Grammar

4 **Write affirmative and negative sentences or questions in the present perfect. Use the verbs in the box.**

become   buy   build   visit   write   learn

1 Lesley / a doctor ?
2 they / New York ?
3 I / a lot of English this year ✓
4 Mark / new sports shoes ✗
5 They / a new factory ✗
6 We / some letters ✓

5 **Write questions and answers with *ever* and *never*.**

1 Have you ever been to Australia?
   No, ...
2 (you) ... ?
   Yes, we've tried Chinese food.
3 Have they ever changed school?
   No, ...
4 (I) ... ?
   Yes, you've met my parents twice.
5 Has your brother ever met a famous person?
   No, ...

Grammar review: Units 1–9

6 **Complete the second sentence so that it means the same as the first sentence. Use the word in brackets in the second sentence.**

I'm going to travel to Paris next weekend. (travelling)
I*'m travelling to* Paris next weekend.

1 I haven't seen the film *Troy*. (never)
   ... the film *Troy*.
2 Paris is smaller than Tokyo. (big)
   Paris ... as Tokyo.
3 You can't smoke in the restaurant. (smoke)
   ... in the restaurant.
4 I met Dave while I was walking in town. (when)
   I was walking in town ... Dave.
5 The TV programmes were bad so we watched a DVD. (because)
   We watched a DVD ... bad.

Revision: Units 7-9

Vocabulary

1 **Complete the sentences about the family.**

1 Your brother's daughter is your … .
2 Your parents' son is your … .
3 Your father's mother is your … .
4 Your mother's sister is your … .
5 Your wife's father is your … .
6 Your aunt's son is your … .

2 **Complete the sentences with the verbs *go, make, do* and *have*.**

1 I always … on foot to school.
2 Let's … a picnic!
3 My mum makes dinner and I … the washing up.
4 I love camping! We always … a barbecue and we … lots of new friends.
5 I always … my homework at 6 p.m.
6 Don't worry if you … a mistake.
7 I usually … a shower first, then I … my bed.
8 Every month we … on a day trip.

3 **Are these verbs positive or negative when we talk about the planet? Complete the table.**

save   recycle   waste   damage
throw away   protect

Positive	Negative

4 **Choose the correct answer.**

1 The beach was very dirty and full of **pollution** / **green**.
2 Put glass things in the **conservation** / **bottle bank**.
3 If we don't look after our **conservation** / **environment**, we'll damage the natural world.
4 Buy things that don't have a lot of **green** / **packaging**.
5 We can all help with the **conservation** / **packaging** of the natural world.
6 She is **pollution** / **green**. At the weekend she works with an organisation that protects plants and trees.

5 **Match the verbs 1–7 with the nouns a–g.**

1 have   a posters
2 wear   b a demonstration
3 sign   c wristbands
4 write   d money
5 go on   e letters
6 put up   f a meeting
7 collect   g a petition

6 **Complete the text with the words in the box.**

subject   rucksack   exam   exercise books
locker   homework   lessons   text books

You need to be strong to go to school! I've got ten big (1) … and I've also got twenty (2)… to write in! I use some of them at school in my (4) … and I use the others at home for my (5) … . I can't take all my books home every day because my … isn't big enough! I leave some of them in my (7) … at school. Tonight I'm taking my science books home because tomorrow I've got a science (8) … . I think science is a very difficult (9) … !

7 **Match the words in the box with the photos 1–4. Use some photos twice.**

woods   hill   cottage   stream   fields   footpath

90

Grammar

1 Write affirmative or negative sentences or questions with *going to*. Replace the time expressions with the dates and times in the box.

> July   Monday 14th June   Saturday 6th June
> ~~Monday 1st June 8 p.m.~~   Tuesday 2nd June 9 a.m.
> Monday 8th June

Today is Monday 1st June.
Emma / watch the new Jude Law film / this evening. ✓
Emma is going to watch the news on TV. (Monday 1st June 8 p.m.)

1 Simon / visit his cousins /next week. ✗
2 Karen / fly to Dublin / next weekend. **?**
3 Charlotte / run ten kilometres / tomorrow morning. ✓
4 I / do a history exam / in two weeks' time. ✗
5 They / go on holiday / next month. **?**

2 What are you doing at the adventure weekend next month? Write affirmative sentences in the present continuous.

We're going horse riding.

next month's adventure weekend

- **Go horse riding**
- **Play football**
- **Go cycling**
- **Have a barbecue**
- **Sing some songs**
- **Sleep in tents**
- **Make some new friends**

3 Write predictions with *will* and *won't*. Use the verbs in the box to write your sentences.

> find   rain   disappear   damage   recycle
> swim   go on

1 People … old clothes and mobile phones more. ✓
2 We … life on other planets. ✗
3 We … the beaches with pollution. ✓
4 Our children … in the sea. ✗
5 Animals … from the planet. ✓
6 People … more demonstrations. ✓
7 It … and there will be more droughts. ✗

4 Write questions with *will* for the answers.

1 … ? Yes, Alice will play in the basketball match.
2 … ? No, they won't come to the meeting.
3 Where … ? The plane will land at Heathrow airport.
4 When … ? He'll arrive at 10 o'clock.
5 … ? Yes, they'll sign the petition.
6 … ? Yes, he'll send an email.

5 Complete the first conditional sentences with the words in the box.

> visit / go   pass / study   not practise / not speak
> buy / cycle   phone / speak   ~~win / buy~~
> be / rain   come / have   not save / not recycle

If I *win* the prize money,
I*'ll buy* a Ferrari.

1 If they … to the picnic, we … a good time.
2 If I…, I … good English.
3 There … floods if it … a lot.
4 If she … , I … to her.
5 If they … Vienna, they … to the museums.
6 We … the planet if we … .
7 If he … a bicycle, he … to school.
8 You … the exam if you … a lot.

6 Complete the imperative sentences with the words in the box. Who is speaking? Choose: A your teacher, B your friends or C your parents.

come   finish   ~~get up~~   eat   send   phone
be   don't   do   write   go

Get up! It's 8 o'clock. *C*

1   … talk in class! Listen to me! …
2   Don't … me tonight. I've got an exam tomorrow morning. …
3   Go to your bedroom and … your homework! …
4   … to my birthday party. You'll have a good time! …
5   … to bed. It's late! …
6   … me a text message about the school trip. …
7   … the exercises you've started on page 25 for homework. …
8   Don't … the dessert now. First eat all your vegetables! …
9   … the words in your exercise books. …
10 Don't … late. Your grandmother is coming for dinner. …

7 Use the information to write affirmative and negative sentences in the present perfect.

	mum	dad	sister
paint a bedroom	✓	✗	✗
meet a famous person	✗	✓	✓
visit the USA	✗	✗	✓
move house	✓	✓	✗

1   My mum … a bedroom.
2   My dad and my sister… a bedroom.
3   My mum … a famous person.
4   My dad and my sister … a famous person.
5   My mum and my dad … the USA.
6   My sister … the USA.
7   My mum and dad … house.
8   My sister … house.

8 Write questions in the present perfect. Use the verbs in the box.

eat   send   buy   read   visit   sail   do

1   you / to New Zealand on a boat
2   you / your homework
3   he / some new trainers
4   we / Chinese food
5   they / the new museum
6   I / a book in English
7   your English friend / you an email

9 Write present perfect questions with *ever* and answers with *never*.

1   you / travel / to Rome?
    No, I / go / to Italy.
2   Darren / meet / your family?
    No, he / visit / my house.
3   they / speak / another language?
    No, they / learn / another language.
4   your brother / make / dinner?
    No, he / cook a meal / in his life.
5   you / win / a competition?
    No, I / enter / a competition.

Consolidation

1 Complete the text. Put the verbs in the correct tense. In the last paragraph, decide which tense to use: present perfect, *going to* or first conditional.

Present perfect
This ... (**1** be) a hard year for me. I'm in the national junior volleyball team and I ... (**2** have) a lot of work at the gym and at school. With all my homework, exams and sports activities I ... (**3** not have) time to see my family or my friends. It ... (**4** not be) easy for my mum and dad but they ... (**5** help) me a lot. This year I ... (**6** make) some great friends in the team and we play well together. We ... (**7** not lose) any games!

Going to
The team ... (**8** play) in the European championship next month and I ... (**9** play) too! My mum and dad ... (**10** not travel) to the championship because it's in Bulgaria, but we ... (**11** speak) on the phone every day.

First conditional
At the championship, If we ... (**12** work) hard, we ... (**13** win) a medal. But if we ... (**14** not win) a medal, I ... (**15** not be) sad.

You decide!
We ... (**16** enjoy) this year and we ... (**17** not have) any problems. ... I ... (**18** play) next year? Well, I don't know. It's a lot of extra work, but if we ... (**19** win) a gold medal in Bulgaria, it ... (**20** be) difficult to say no!

2 There is a mistake in each sentence. Find the mistakes and correct them.

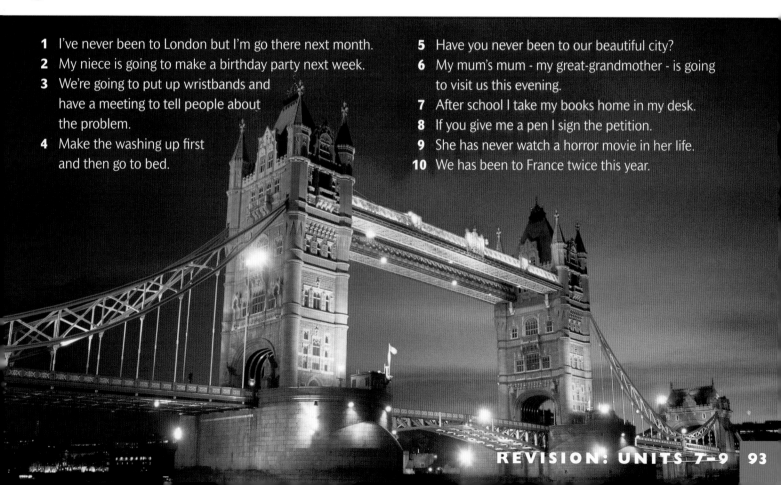

1 I've never been to London but I'm go there next month.
2 My niece is going to make a birthday party next week.
3 We're going to put up wristbands and have a meeting to tell people about the problem.
4 Make the washing up first and then go to bed.
5 Have you never been to our beautiful city?
6 My mum's mum - my great-grandmother - is going to visit us this evening.
7 After school I take my books home in my desk.
8 If you give me a pen I sign the petition.
9 She has never watch a horror movie in her life.
10 We has been to France twice this year.

Pronunciation

Getting started
The phonetic alphabet

1 💿 **Listen and repeat the words.**

/i:/	meat	/ɒ/	want	/aɪ/	nine
/ɪ/	did	/ɔ:/	more	/ɔɪ/	boy
/e/	ten	/ʊ/	look	/aʊ/	how
/æ/	cat	/u:/	Sue	/əʊ/	don't
/ɑ:/	car	/ɜ:/	girl	/eə/	hair
/ʌ/	cup	/eɪ/	day	/ɪə/	here

2 **Add these words to the list in exercise 1 according to their vowel sounds.**

good   run   first   need   dad   out
pray   near   go   not   send   dark
two   there   right   four   give   toy

3 **Complete these words with the correct symbol.**

/m...d/	made	/sn.../	snow
/w...z/	was	/s...d/	said
/br...t/	brought	/f...m/	farm
/sk...l/	school	/j.../	year
/f...v/	five	/h...m/	him

4 💿 **Listen and repeat the words.**

/b/	big	/ʒ/	leisure	/ŋ/	sing
/d/	dog	/v/	very	/j/	yesterday
/t/	to	/dʒ/	jacket	/h/	how
/p/	pen	/f/	from	/m/	man
/g/	good	/ð/	this	/n/	never
/k/	come	/θ/	fourth	/l/	like
/ʃ/	she	/s/	six	/r/	red
/tʃ/	March	/z/	zoo	/w/	went

5 **Write the correct symbol above the highlighted consonants in these sentences.**

A   My dad likes Italian food.
B   We want to buy a new car.

Unit 1 The sounds /s/, /z/ and /iz/

Present simple 3rd person endings

1 💿 **Listen to the first sound in the words. Can you hear the difference? Practise saying them.**

2 💿 **Listen to the sentences and repeat.**

3 **Put the verbs below into three groups depending on the pronunciation of the third person ending.**

goes   finishes   stops   has   does   walks
watches   wants   uses   tries   changes   speaks

Group 1 /s/	Group 2 /z/	Group 3 /iz/
	goes	

4 **Practise saying the words with another student.**

Unit 2 The sounds /n/ and /ŋ/

1 Look at the words below. Check the meaning of new words in the dictionary or with your teacher.

2 🔘 Listen and underline the word you hear.

	/n/	/ŋ/
a	thin	thing
b	win	wing
c	keen	king
d	pain	paying
e	sin	sing
f	Ron	wrong

3 Listen again and practise saying the pairs of words.

4 Practise reading the sentences with a partner.

a Simon is living in Hong Kong.
b Boring Ron isn't having fun.
c What songs are you playing at the concert this evening?
d Dan is running in a competition.
e Justin is learning to sing.

Unit 3 Sentence stress and rhythm

Comparative sentences

1 🔘 Listen and write the sentences you hear a–e.

2 In the sentences from exercise 1 some words are strong and some words are weak. The important words are strong and the others are weak. With your partner decide which are the important (strong) words.

3 🔘 Listen again and mark the strong words.

•   •   •
Anna is younger than Jane.

4 Practise saying the sentences. Try to say the weak words as quickly as you can.

Unit 4 Past tense endings

1 Write the past tense of the verbs in the table.

	Present	Past	Number of syllables
a	look	*looked*	*1 syllable*
b	want	*wanted*	*2 syllables*
c	laugh	_____	_____
d	stop	_____	_____
e	shout	_____	_____
f	need	_____	_____
g	walk	_____	_____
h	move	_____	_____
i	hate	_____	_____
j	watch	_____	_____

2 Write the number of syllables in the past tense in the table.

3 🔘 Listen, check and repeat.

4 Can you complete the pronunciation rule?

We add an extra syllable in the past tense if the present tense ends in ___ or ___ .

5 🔘 Listen and underline the verb you hear, past or present.

a They like / liked the game.
b I love / loved playing volleyball.
c We laugh / laughed a lot.
d I need / needed an ice cream

6 Practise saying the sentences with a partner.

Unit 5 Intonation

1 Listen to the questions about last weekend. Does the person sound interested or bored?

Tick (✓) the correct column.

Last weekend …

	interested ☺	bored ☹
a 1 Did you go shopping?		
2 Did you go shopping?		
b 1 Did you watch TV?		
2 Did you watch TV?		
c 1 Where did you go?		
2 Where did you go?		
d 1 What did you do?		
2 What did you do?		

There are two types of question:

Yes/No questions where the answer is yes or no.
E.g. Do you like bananas? Yes, I do. / No, I don't.

And *Wh- questions* which begin with a question word (What, When, Where, How, Who etc).
E.g. Where do you live?

2 Listen to the questions. Does the intonation go up ↑ or down ↓?

a Did you go shopping?
b Did you watch TV?
c Where did you go?
d What did you do?

3 Underline the correct word in the sentences to complete the rule.

In *Yes/No questions* the intonation goes up / down.

In *Wh- questions* the intonation goes up / down.

4 Listen again and practise asking the questions. Make sure you sound interested!

5 Ask and answer the questions with your partner.

Unit 6 Word stress

1 Listen to the words and answer the questions.

anxious   grateful

a How many syllables do the words have?
b Is the second syllable strong or weak?

2 Listen to the words in the box and underline the strong or stressed syllable.

anxious   grateful   afraid   upset   desperate
relaxed   ashamed   enthusiastic

3 Listen and write the questions that you hear.

4 Ask and answer the questions with a partner.

Unit 7 Final consonants

1 Look at the words below. Check the meaning of new words in the dictionary or with your teacher.

	A	B		A	B
1	goal	gold	6	your	York
2	ten	tenth	7	four	fourth
3	hole	hold	8	pass	passed
4	bell	belt	9	nest	next
5	when	went	10	word	work

2 Listen and write the word you hear.

3 Practise saying the words with a partner. When you say the words in B, make sure you say the sounds in bold very clearly.

4 Listen and write the sentences that you hear.

5 Listen again and repeat the questions.

6 Ask and answer the questions with your partner.

Unit 8 Sounds and spelling

The letter 'a'

We pronounce the letter 'a' in many different ways.

1 🔊 **Listen and practise saying the sounds.**

a /æ/ cat
b /ɑ:/ bath
c /eɪ/ paper
d /ɪ/ village
e /ɔ:/ small

2 **Which word has a different sound?**

a	stay	bag	waste
b	bank	have	supermarket
c	snack	father	glass
d	damage	packaging	make
e	charity	all	water

3 🔊 **Listen, check and then repeat.**

4 **Write the words in exercise 2 in the correct box below.**

1 /æ/ cat	2 /ɑ:/ bath	3 /eɪ/ paper	4 /ɪ/ village	5 /ɔ:/ small
		stay		

5 🔊 **Listen and check, then practise saying the words.**

Unit 9 Short forms

In conversation, we usually use short forms. So we say *I'll go* and not *I will go*.

1 **Write the sentences again, using short forms.**

I have got two brothers.
I've got two brothers.

a I will do my homework later.
b She has got a pink ipod.
c They have never been to London.
d I am from Tokyo.
e He is very moody.
f What is your name?
g We are going to the beach.
h He will meet you in the café.

2 🔊 **Listen to the sentences and practise saying them. Pay attention to the pronunciation of the short forms.**

Grammar reference

Getting started

to be

Affirmative
I**'m** at the gym.
I **am** at the gym.
You**'re** at the gym.
You **are** at the gym.
He**'s**/She**'s**/It**'s** at the gym.
He/She/It **is** at the gym.
We**'re**/You**'re**/They**'re** at the gym.
We/You/They **are** at the gym.

Negative
I**'m not** good
I **am not** good.
You **aren't** good.
You **are not** good.
He/She/It **isn't** good.
He/She/It **is not** good.
We/You/They **aren't** good.
We/You/They **are not** good.

Questions
Am I happy?
Are you happy?
Is he/she/it happy?
Are we/you/they happy?

Short answers	
Yes, I **am**.	No, I**'m not**.
Yes, you **are**.	No, you **aren't**.
Yes, he/she/it **is**.	No, he/she/it **isn't**.
Yes, we/you/they **are**.	No, we/you/they **aren't**.

have got

Affirmative and negative
I**'ve got** a car.
You **have got** a car.
You **haven't got** a car.
He**'s**/She**'s**/It**'s got** a car.
He/She/It **has got** a car.
He/She/It **hasn't got** a car.
We**'ve**/You**'ve**/They**'ve got** a car.
We/You/They **have got** a car.
We/You/They **haven't got** a car.

Questions
Have I **got** an MP3 player?
Have you **got** an MP3 player?
Has he/she/it **got** an MP3 player?
Have we/you/they **got** an MP3 player?

Short answers	
Yes, I **have**.	No, I **haven't**.
Yes, you **have**.	No, you **haven't**.
Yes, he/she/it **has**.	No, he/he/it **hasn't**.
Yes, we/you/they **have**.	No, we/you/they **haven't**.

Form

- We use *is* to make the third person singular of *to be*. We use *has* to make the third person singular of *have got*.
  *Mrs Manley **is** our school PE teacher.*
  *Lisa **has got** an MP3 player.*

- We use **not** to make the negative forms of *to be* and *have got*.
  *I**'m not** interested in volleyball.*
  *She **hasn't got** a sister.*

- We invert the subject and verb to make questions.
  ***Are you** interested in volleyball?*
  ***Have they got** a big garden?*

Use

- We can use *to be* with nouns, adjectives and prepositions.
  be + noun:
  She's the teacher. I'm a student.
  be + adjective:
  Maths is important. I'm interested in gymnastics.
  be + preposition:
  They're in the computer room. We're from New York.

- We use *have got* to talk about possession.
  I've got a computer in my bedroom.
  My brother hasn't got a mobile phone.

- We use *to be*, not *have got*, to talk about age.
  I'm fourteen years old.
  (not I've got fourteen years old.)
  You're twenty-five. (not You've got twenty-five.)

- We use *to be*, not *have got*, to talk about feelings.
  I'm cold. (not I've got cold.)
  He's hungry. (not He's got hungry.)

Pronouns and adjectives

Subject pronoun
I've got a CD.
I've got some CDs.
You've got a bag.
You've got three bags.
He's got a car.
He's got two cars.
She's got a DVD.
She's got five DVDs.
We've got a house.
We've got two houses.
You've got a book.
You've got some books.
They've got a bike.
They've got four bikes.

Possessive adjective
It's **my** CD.
They're **my** CDs.
It's **your** bag.
They're **your** bags.
It's **his** car.
They're **his** cars.
It's **her** DVD.
They're **her** DVDs.
It's **our** house.
They're **our** houses.
It's **your** book.
They're **your** books.
It's **their** bike.
They're **their** bikes.

Possessive pronoun
The CD is **mine**.
The CDs are **mine**.
The bag is **yours**.
The bags are **yours**
The car is **his**.
The cars are **his**.
The DVD is **hers**.
The DVDs are **hers**.
The house is **ours**.
The houses are **ours**.
The book is **yours**.
The books are **yours**.
The bike is **theirs**.
The bikes are **theirs**.

Possessive 's

Form

- We use 's after a name or noun.
  *He is **Kate's** brother.*
- We add ' after a plural noun ending in s.
  *It is my **cousins'** computer.*

Use

- Talking about possession.
  *The **students'** classroom is big.*
  ***Naomi's** bike is new.*

Affirmative
There's a lamp.
There is a lamp.
There are some books.

Negative
There isn't a photo.
There aren't any CDs.

Questions
Is there a DVD?
Are there any beds?

Short answers	
Yes, **there is.**	No, **there isn't.**
Yes, **there are.**	No, **there aren't.**

Articles

- We use *a* before nouns that begin with a consonant sound.
  a bed   a class   a house   a subject
- We use *an* before nouns that begin with a vowel sound.
  an apple   an egg   an orange   an uncle
- We use *the* to refer to one specific thing or person. The listener knows the thing or person we mean.
  The science teacher** is in the classroom. **(You know the teacher.)
  *You can use **the computer**. **(You know the computer.)***
- We use *a* and *an* when the listener doesn't know which thing or person we mean, or when it doesn't matter.
  *I eat **an apple** for breakfast. **(It doesn't matter which apple.)***
  *He's got **a poster** of an elephant. **(You don't know the poster.)***
- We use *a* and *an* to talk about people's jobs.
  *Their mum is **a doctor**.*
  *He's **a teacher**.*

Unit 1

Present simple

Affirmative
I/You play basketball.
He/she/it play**s** basketball.
We/You/They play basketball.

Negative	
Short form	*Long form*
I/You **don't** study.	I/You **do not** study.
He/she/it **doesn't** study.	He/she/it **does not** study.
We/You/They **don't** study.	We/You/They **do not** study.

Questions
Do I/you go to school?
Does he/she/it go to school?
Do we/you/they go to school?

Short answers	
Yes, I/you **do**.	No, I/you **don't**.
Yes, he/she/it **does**.	No, he/she/it **doesn't**.
Yes, we/you/they **do**.	Yes, we/you/they **don't**.

Form

- Affirmative: Subject + infinitive
  *He **listens** to music.*
- Negative: Subject + *don't/doesn't* + infinitive
  *We **don't study** in the same class.*
- Questions: *Do/does* + subject + infinitive ?
  ***Do** they **go** to the same school?*
  *What **does** Mark **love**?*

Spelling: 3rd person singular

- In affirmative sentences, for 3rd person singular (*he/she/it*) we add *s*.
  play   ➔   Kelly plays volleyball.
- Verbs ending in consonant + *y*: replace *y* with *ies*.
  try   ➔   He tries to help other people.
- Verbs ending in *ss, ch, sh, x, o*: add *es*.
  go   ➔   He goes everywhere in a wheelchair.
- *Be* and *have* are irregular.
  be   ➔   He is good at listening.
  have   ➔   He always has time for his friends.

Use

- Talking about routines and repeated actions:
  *What **do** we **do** at home?*
  *After school we always **play** football.*
- Talking about likes and opinions:
  *We **don't like** the same subjects.*
  *People **think** he's unfriendly.*

Adverbs of frequency

never	sometimes	often	usually	always
0%	50%	75%	90%	100%

Form

- We put adverbs of frequency after the verb *to be*.
  *I'm **sometimes** selfish.*
- We put adverbs of frequency before other verbs.
  *He **always has** time for his friends.*

Use

- Talking about frequency
  *Mark **never** gives up.*
  *We **often** go to the gym.*

Object pronouns

Subject pronouns	Object pronouns
I'm Sally.	Mark is a good example for **me**.
You play volleyball.	Maria plays with **you**.
He's my twin brother.	I'm more intelligent than **him**.
She's at the gym.	I've got gymnastics with **her**.
It's David's computer.	He plays on **it**.
We're twins.	It's easy for **us**.
You are the students.	Is it clear to **you**?
They are his friends.	He tries to help **them**.

Form

- We put object pronouns after the verb.
  *I **admire him**.*
- Prepositions often go before object pronouns.
  *Our mother looks **at us**.*

Use

- The object of a verb can be a name, a noun, or an object pronoun.
  *I play basketball with **Mark**.* ➜ *I play basketball with **him**.*
  *He plays on **the computer**.* ➜ *He plays on **it**.*

Question words

Use

- **What**: asking about things
  ***What** does he like? History and languages.*
- **Which + noun**: asking about a limited number of things
  ***Which subject** do they like? PE.*
- **Who**: asking about people
  ***Who** do you admire? My friend Mark.*
  ***Who** does she speak to? Mark.*
- **Where**: asking about places
  ***Where** does she play volleyball? At the gym.*
- **When**: asking about times and dates
  ***When** do you go to the gym? On Thursdays.*
- **Why**: asking for reasons
  ***Why** do I admire Mark? Because he never gives up.*
- **How often**: asking about frequency
  ***How often** does she play basketball? Never.*

Unit 2

Present continuous

Affirmative

Short form	Long form
I **'m** jogging.	I **am** jogging.
You**'re** jogging.	You **are** jogging.
He**'s**/She**'s**/It**'s** jogging.	He/She/It **is** jogging.
We**'re** jogging.	We **are** jogging.
You**'re** jogging.	You **are** jogging.
They**'re** jogging.	They **are** jogging.

Negative

Short form	Long form
I**'m not** acting.	I **am not** acting.
You **aren't** acting.	You **are not** acting.
He/She/It **isn't** acting.	He/She/It **is not** acting.
We **aren't** acting.	We **are not** acting.
You **aren't** acting.	You **are not** acting.
They **aren't** acting.	They **are not** acting.

Questions

Questions
Am I record**ing** a CD?
Are you record**ing** a CD?
Is he/she/it record**ing** a CD?
Are we/you/they record**ing** a CD?

Short answers

Short answers	
Yes, I **am**.	No, I **'m not**.
Yes, you **are**.	No, you **aren't**.
Yes, he/she/it **does**.	No, he/she/it **isn't**.
Yes, we/you/they **do**.	No, we **aren't**.

Form

- *to be + ing* form
  Sara **is working** hard.
  We **aren't playing** football.
  What other things **are** you **doing**?

Spelling: -*ing* form

- We add -*ing* to the infinitive of most verbs.
  play ➔ We aren't play**ing** today.
- Verbs ending in *e*: replace *e* with -*ing*.
  make ➔ We're mak**ing** a web page.
- Verbs ending in one vowel and one consonant: **double consonant** + -*ing*.
  jog ➔ We're jo**gging**.

Use

- Talking about actions that are happening at the moment:
  What **are** you **doing** at the moment?
  This week she**'s doing** school exams.

Present simple or present continuous?

- We use the present simple to talk about activities that usually happen.
  We **study** music and we also **study** normal school subjects.
  We **do** lots of sports at school.
- We often use adverbs and expressions of frequency with the present simple.
  I **usually play** football.
  We **always study** Shakespeare on Fridays.
- We use the present continuous to talk about activities that are happening now.
  We**'re rehearsing** for our European tour.
  What **are** you **doing**? We're jogging. (**not** ~~What do you do?~~)
- We often use expressions like *today*, *now*, or *at the moment* with the present continuous.
  We **aren't playing** football **today**.
  This week we**'re making** a web page.

Unit 3

Comparatives and superlatives

Adjective	
1 syllable	clean
	tall
1 syllable (ending in	thin
1 vowel + 1 consonant	hot
2 syllables (ending in y)	friendly
	sunny
2 or more syllables	expensive
	interesting
irregular	good
	bad
	far

Comparative	
add er	cleaner
	taller
double consonant,	hotter
add er	thinner
replace y with ier	friendlier
	sunnier
more + adjective	more expensive
	more interesting
	better
	worse
	further

Superlative	
the + add est	the cleanest
	the tallest
the + double	the thinnest
consonant, add est	the hottest
the + replace y	the friendliest
with iest	the sunniest
the most + adjective	the most expensive
	the most interesting
	the best
	the worst
	the furthest

Form

- In comparative sentences, we use *than* (not *that*).
  *They do more exciting activities **than** watching TV. (**not** ~~more exciting activities that watching TV~~)*
  *Cable TV is better **than** Public TV. (**not** ~~better that Public TV~~)*
- We put *the* before superlative adjectives.
  *They show **the** funniest programmes.*
  ***The** best programmes are Manga cartoons.*
- In superlative sentences, we use *in* (not *of*) with places.
  *They are the biggest TV watchers **in** the world. (**not** ~~the biggest TV watchers of the world~~)*
  *The Mojave desert is the hottest place **in** the world. (**not** ~~the hottest place of the world~~)*

Use

- We use the comparative to compare two things, people or groups.
  The Swedes are happier than other nationalities.
  TV is more popular in America than in Britain.
- We use the superlative to compare three or more things or people.
  Watching TV is the coolest free time activity.

Negative comparisons

- We can make negative comparisons with *not as* + adjective + *as*.
  *It isn't as interesting **as** a documentary.*
  *In Sweden, TV is**n't as** popular **as** it is in the other countries.*

can

Affirmative
I/You/He/She/It/We/You/They **can** make films.

Negative
I/You/He/She/It/We/You/They **can't** make films.

Questions
Can I/you/he/she/it/we/you/they make films?

Short answers
Yes, I/You/He/She/It/We/You/They **can**.
No, I/You/He/She/It/We/You/They **can't**.

Form

- In questions, we invert the subject and *can*.
  Can you make a film with £1000? (**not** ~~Do you can make a film~~)

Use

- Talking about talents and abilities:
  Can you make films? Yes, I can.
- Talking about possiblities:
  Can you make a film with only £1000?

must

Affirmative
I/You/He/She/It/We/You/They **must** finish your dinner.

Negative
I/You/He/She/It/We/You/They **mustn't** arrive late.

Form

- After *must* and *mustn't*, we use the infinitive without *to*.
  You **must finish** *your dinner.*(**not** ~~You must to finish your dinner.~~)

Use

- Talking about obligations:
  You **mustn't** *arrive late.*
  You **must** *do your homework.*
- Giving strong advice:
  You **must** *look for a good location.*

Past simple: *be*

Affirmative
I **was** happy.
You **were** happy.
He/She/It **was** happy.
We/You/They **were** happy.

Negative
I **wasn't** happy.
You **weren't** happy.
He/she/it **wasn't** happy.
We/You/They **weren't** happy.

Questions
Was I happy?
Were you happy?
Was he/she/it happy?
Were we/you/they we happy?

Short answers	
Yes, I **was**.	No, I **wasn't**.
Yes, you **were**.	No, you **weren't**.
Yes, he/she/it **was**.	No, he/she/it **wasn't**.
Yes, we/you/they **were**.	No, we/you/they **weren't**.

Past simple: *can*

Affirmative
I/You/He/She/It/We/You/They **could** talk.

Negative
I/You/He/She/It/We/You/They **couldn't** talk.

Questions
Could I/you/he/she/it/we/you/they talk?

Short answers
Yes, I/you/he/she/it/we/you/they **could**.
No, I/you/he/she/it/we/you/they **couldn't**.

Unit 4

Past simple

Affirmative
I/You/He/She/It/We/You/They arriv**ed** on 20th July.
I/You/He/She/It/We/You/They went on 20th July.

Negative
Short form
I/You/He/She/It/We/You/They **didn't** arrive.
I/You/He/She/It/We/You/They **didn't** go.
Long form
I/You/He/She/It/We/You/They **did not** arrive.
I/You/He/She/It/We/You/They **did not** go.

Questions
Did I/you/he/she/it/we/you/they arrive?
Did I/you/he/she/it/we/you/they go?

Short answers
Yes, I/you/he/she/it/we/you/they **did**.
No, I/you/he/she/it/we/you/they **didn't**.

Form

- Affirmative (regular verbs): Subject + verb with *ed*
  She laughed.
- Affirmative (irregular verbs): Subject + irregular past form
  We went through the doors.
- Negative: Subject + *didn't* + infinitive
  I didn't have the tickets.
- Questions: *Did* + subject + infinitive ?
  Did you remember the tickets?

Spelling: regular verbs

- In affirmative sentences, for most regular verbs we add *ed*.
  shout ➔ *Suzy shouted.*
- Verbs ending in *e*: add *d*.
  move ➔ *The blue colour moved like the sea.*
- Verbs ending in consonant + *y*: replace *y* with *ied*.
  hurry ➔ *She hurried because she was late.*
- Verbs ending in 1 vowel and 1 consonant: **double consonant** + *ed*.
  travel ➔ *Three astronauts travelled on the spaceship.*

Irregular verbs

- In affirmative sentences, many verbs have an irregular form. There is a list of irregular verbs on page 119.
  run ➔ *We **ran** across to the check-in desk.*
  give ➔ *Suzy **gave** them to the check-in assistant.*
  get ➔ *We **got** on the plane.*
  make ➔ *Someone **made** a film in a studio.*
- In negative sentences, we use *didn't* and the infinitive with all verbs.
  *I **didn't bring** my passport. (**not** I didn't brought my passport.)*
- In questions, we use *did* and the infinitive with all verbs.
  *Did you **see** her hands? (**not** Did you saw her hands?)*

Use

- Talking about an event that finished in the past:
  *Man **arrived** on the moon on 20th July 1969.*
  *Collins **didn't leave** the Apollo.*

Unit 5

Past simple

See Unit 4 on page 105.

Countable and uncountable nouns

Affirmative	
Countable	He worked in **a** factory.
	He started **an** organisation.
	Some schools helped.
Uncountable	They collected **some** money.

Negative	
Countable	They didn't have any books.
Uncountable	They didn't have **any** paper.

Questions	
Countable	Did I see **any** schools?
Uncountable	Did they have **any** food?

Form

• In affirmative sentences, we use *some* (not *a* or *an*) with uncountable nouns.
  We had some good weather. (**not** ~~We had a good weather.~~)
• Uncountable nouns do not normally have a plural form.
  There was some food and water. (**not** ~~some foods and waters.~~)

Use

• Some nouns are countable. They can be singular and plural.
  *Iqbal Masih worked in **a factory**.* ➡ *The children worked all day in **factories**.*
  A shark attacked her. ➡ *Suddenly some **sharks** appeared.*
• Some nouns are uncountable. We don't normally count them, and they can't normally be plural.
  *They collected some **money**.*
  *We had good **weather**.*

Unit 6

Past continuous

Affirmative
I **was** runn**ing**.
You **were** runn**ing**.
He/she/it **was** runn**ing**.
We/You/They **were** runn**ing**.

Negative	
Short form	*Long form*
I **wasn't** moving.	I **was not** moving.
You **weren't** moving.	You **were not** moving.
He/she/it **wasn't** moving.	He/she/it **was not** moving.
We **weren't** moving.	We **were not** moving.
You **weren't** moving.	You **were not** moving.
They **weren't** moving.	They **were not** moving.

Questions
Was I looking?
Were you looking?
Was he/she/it looking?
Were we/you/they looking?

Short answers	
Yes, I **was**.	No, I **wasn't**.
Yes, you **were**.	No, you **weren't**.
Yes, he/she/it **was**.	No, he/she/it **wasn't**.
Yes, we/you/they **were**.	No, we/you/they **weren't**.

Form

• Affirmative: Subject + *was/were* + *ing* form
  *Big waves **were** form**ing**.*
• Negative: Subject + *wasn't/weren't* + *ing* form
  *The tourists **weren't** moving from the beach.*
• Questions: *Was/were* + subject + *ing* form ?
  ***Was** Dave walk**ing** fast?*
  *Where **was** he go**ing**?*

Spelling: -*ing* form

See Unit 2 Present continuous on page 102.

Use

• Talking about actions that were in progress at a specific time in the past:
  *Tilly **was** sunbath**ing** on Maikhao beach.*
  *What **was** happen**ing**?*

Past simple or past continuous?

- We use the past simple to talk about actions that finished at a specific time in the past.
  *On 26 December 2004 the sea suddenly **disappeared**.*
  *The tsunami **didn't kill** anybody on Maikhao beach.*
- We use the past continuous to describe actions or situations that were in progress, but not completed, at a specific time in the past.
  *The waves **were destroying** the small tourist centre.*
  *Everybody **was running** to the top floor.*
- We use the past continuous to talk about a longer action, and the past simple to talk about a shorter action that interrupts.
  *While big waves **were forming**, the tourists **watched**.*
  *Dave **was walking** slowly when he **saw** a village.*
- We can use the past continuous to describe a scene, and the past simple to describe a sequence of actions.
  *The bears **were fishing** and **eating** salmon. They **didn't see** him, so Dave **continued** along the river.*

Unit 7

Future forms: *going to*

Affirmative
I'm going to stay at home.
You're going to stay at home.
He/She/It**'s** going to stay at home.
We're/You're/They're going to stay at home.

Negative
I'm not going to enjoy it.
You **aren't** going to enjoy it.
He/She/It **isn't** going to enjoy it.
We/You/They **aren't** going to enjoy it.

Questions
Am I **going to** study?
Are you **going to** study?
Is he/she/it **going to** study?
Are we/you/they **going to** study?

Short answers	
Yes, I **am**.	No, **I'm not**.
Yes, you **are**.	No, you **aren't**.
Yes, he/she/it **is**.	No, he/she/it **isn't**.
Yes, we/you/they **are**.	No, we/you/they **aren't**.

Form

- *be + going to* + infinitive
  We're going to study English in the mornings.
  We're not going to play football all day.
  What are we going to do?

Use

- Talking about decisions, plans and intentions for the future:
  *My grandparents **are going to travel** from Australia.*
  *I'm frightened, but **I'm not going to tell** the others.*
- Talking about things in the future that are already decided, or that we think are certain:
  ***I'm not going to enjoy** it.*
  *It **isn't going to be** boring.*

Future forms: Present continuous

Form

See Unit 2 Present continuous on page 102.

Use

- We can use the present continuous to talk about definite plans and arrangements for the near future, especially when they include a time, a place, or other people.
  We're having a big exam tomorrow.
  They're sending me to a brat camp this summer.
- We don't use the present simple to talk about the future.
  Lots of friends and family are coming to the picnic. (not Lots of friends and family come to the picnic.)
- There is often no difference between the present continuous and *going to*.
  Next week we're going to visit a theme park.
  = Next week we're visiting a theme park.
  What are you going to do for your end-of-year school trip?
  = What are you doing for your end-of-year school trip?
- We usually use the present continuous, not *going to*, with the verbs *come* and *go*.
  My grandparents are coming from Sydney next week.
  I'm not going to the beach this summer.

Unit 8

Future forms: *will*

Affirmative
I'll/You'll/He'll/She'll/It'll/We'll/You'll/They'll help.

Negative
I/You/He/She/It/We/You/They **won't** help.

Questions
Will I/you/he/she/it/we/you/they help?

Short answers
Yes, I/you/he/she/it/we/you/they **will**.
No, I/you/he/she/it/we/you/they **won't**.

Form

- *will/won't* + infinitive
  There will be food for the tigers.
  They won't enter villages looking for food.
  Will our planet survive?

Use

- Making predictions about the future:
  Soon, it'll be too late.
  Tigers won't survive in the modern world.
- Making future predictions with *think* or *probably*:
  I think our team will win the league next year.
  My classmate Emma will probably go to university at eighteen.

First conditional

Condition	Consequence
If you **have** a shower,	you'll use less water.
If more tigers **die**,	they will disappear from the planet.

Form

- *If* + present simple + *will*
  or
  will + *if* + present simple
  If you have a shower, you'll use less water.
  You'll use less water if you have a shower.
- When we start the sentence with *If*, we use a comma after the present simple.
  If more tigers die, they'll disappear from our planet.
- We use the present simple (not *will*) after *if*.
  If this continues, the world will have problems. (not If this will continue)

Use

- Talking about possible situations in the future, and the consequences of those situations:
  *If the rainforest **becomes** smaller, there **will be** floods.*
  *We **won't have** new medicines **if** we **destroy** the plants.*

The imperative

Form

- Affirmative: infinitive
  Send us your name and address.
- Negative: *don't* + infinitive
  Don't wait!

Use

- Telling people what to do:
  Don't have a bath, have a shower!
  Think before you buy.

Unit 9

Present perfect

Affirmative

Short form	Long form
I've/You've changed.	I/You have changed.
He's/She's/It's changed.	He/She/It has changed.
We've changed.	We have changed.
You've changed.	You have changed.
They've changed.	They have changed.
I've/You've eaten.	I/You have eaten.
He's/She's/It's eaten.	He/She/It has eaten.
We've eaten.	We have eaten.
You've eaten.	You have eaten.
They've eaten.	They have eaten.

Negative

Short form	Long form
I/You haven't changed.	I/You have not changed.
He/She/It hasn't changed.	He/She/It has not changed.
We haven't changed.	We have not changed.
You haven't changed.	You have notchanged.
They haven't changed.	They have not changed.
I/You haven't eaten.	I/You have not eaten.
He/She/It hasn't eaten.	He/She/It has not eaten.
We haven't eaten.	We have not eaten.
You haven't eaten.	You have not eaten.
They haven't eaten.	They have not eaten.

Questions

Have I/You ask**ed** them?
Have I/You spoken to them?
Has he/she/it ask**ed** them?
Has he/she/it spoken to them?
Have we/you/they ask**ed** them?
Have we/you/they spoken to them?

Short answers

Yes, I/you **have**.	No, I/you **haven't**.
Yes, he/she/it **has**.	No, he/she/it **hasn't**.
Yes, we/you/they **have**.	No, we/you/they **haven't**.

Form

- *has/have* + past participle
  *I've **started** wearing skirts.*
  *My bedroom **hasn't changed**.*
  ***Have** your parents **painted** your bedroom?*

Spelling: regular past participles

- Regular past participles end in *ed*. The spelling rules are the same as for the past simple. See page 105, Unit 4 Past simple.

Irregular past participles

- Many verbs have irregular past participles. There is a list of irregular verbs on page 119.

  be   →   *It' always **been** very untidy.*
  put   →   *I've **put** my desk next to the window.*
  see   →   *They've never **seen** a red and white bedroom.*
  win   →   *He's **won** two Olympic medals.*

Use

- Talking about recent changes that affect the present:
  *I've **changed** my hairstyle. (**It's different now.**)*
  *I've **put** up some new posters. (**They're on the wall now.**)*
- Talking about actions in a period of time that hasn't finished:
  ***This year** Stan **has won** five Olympic medals. (**This year hasn't finished.**)*
  ***Have** you **seen** your cousins **this week**? (**This week hasn't finished.**)*
- Talking about past experiences in our life, when we don't mention a specific time or date:
  *We've **made** lots of friends around the world.*
  *I've **studied** Japanese.*

ever and *never*

- We often use *ever* in present perfect questions to say 'at any time in your life'.
  ***Have** you **ever wanted** to change your life?*
  ***Have** your parents **ever painted** your bedroom?*
- We often use *never* in present perfect sentences to say 'at no time in your life'.
  *They've **never seen** a red and white bedroom.*
  *They've **never been** to secondary school.*

Vocabulary

Getting started

Nouns

art /ɑːt/
chair /tʃeə(r)/
chemist /'kemɪst/
clock /klɒk/
computer programming /kəm'pjuːtə ˌprəʊɡræmɪŋ/
computer studies /kəm'pjuːtə ˌstʌdiz /
course /kɔːs/ take (a) course in sth
dessert /dɪzɜːt/
desk /desk/
floor /flɔː/
genius /'dʒiːniəs/ be a genius (pl geniuses)
geography /dʒi 'ɒɡrəfi/
gym /dʒɪm/
gymnastics /dʒɪm'næstɪks/
lamp /læmp/
maths /mæθs/
meal /miːl/
medal /'medl/ win a medal for (doing) sth
medicine /'medsn/ adj: medical
object /'ɒbdʒekt/
poster /'pəʊstə(r)/
racket /'rækɪt/
result /rɪ'zʌlt/ get the results of sth
river /'rɪvə(r)/
science /'saɪəns/
starter /'stɑːtə(r)/
subject /'sʌbdʒekt/
town /taʊn/
vase / vɑːz/
visitor /'vɪzɪtə(r)/ v: visit
volleyball /'vɒlibɔːl/
wall /wɔːl/
website /'websaɪt/

Verbs

brush / brʌʃ/ n: brush
copy /'kɒpi/ (pt, pp copied)
design /dɪ'zaɪn/ n: design; designer
hear /hɪə(r)/ (pt, pp heard)
leave /liːv/ leave sth somewhere
look /lʊk/
mean /miːn/ (pt, pp meant)
open / 'əʊpən/
relax /rɪ'læks/ n: relaxation
repeat /rɪ'piːt/ n: repetition
send /send/ send (sth/ an email) to sb/somewhere

Adjectives

aloud /ə'laʊd/ opp: silently
boring /'bɔːrɪŋ/ opp: interesting
fantastic /fæn'tæstɪk/
important /ɪm 'pɔːtənt/ important for sth. opp: unimportant
interested /'ɪntrəstɪd/ interested in sth

Phrasal verbs

hand in   hand sth in

Prepositions of place

behind /bɪ'haɪnd/ opp: in front of
in /ɪn/ opp: out (of)
in front of /ɪn 'frʌnt ɒv/ opp: behind
next to /'nekst tuː/
on /ɒn/ opp: under
under /'ʌndə/ opp: on

Unit 1

Nouns

apostrophe /ə'pɒstrəfiː/
atmosphere /'ætməsfɪə(r)/ have an atmosphere
bin /bɪn/
board /bɔːd/
clothes /kləʊðz/
comma /'kɒmə/
dictionary /'dɪkʃənri/ (pl dictionaries)
exam /ɪɡ'zæm/ v: examine
facility /fə'sɪləti/ (pl facilities)
full stop /ˌfʊl 'stɒp/
idea /aɪ'dɪə/ have an idea (about sth)
match /mætʃ/ play a match against sb (pl matches)
opportunity /ˌɒpə'tjuːnəti/ have the opportunity for /
     to do sth (pl opportunities)
power /'paʊə(r)/ adj: powerful
quiz /kwɪz/ (pl quizzes)
shelf /ʃelf/ (pl shelves)
wristband /'rɪstbænd/ wear a wristband

Verbs

admire /əd'maɪə(r)/ n: admirer
ask /ɑːsk/
become /bɪ'kʌm/ (pt, pp became)
begin /bɪ'ɡɪn/ (pt, pp began)
change /tʃeɪndʒ/
check /tʃek/
continue /kən'tɪnjuː/
describe /dɪ'skraɪb/ n: description
finish /'fɪnɪʃ/
give /ɡɪv/ (pt, gave; pp given)

introduce /ˌɪntrə'djuːs/ *n:* introduction
learn /lɜːn/
need /niːd/
offer /'ɒfə(r)/ offer to do sth (for sb)
say /seɪ/ (*pt, pp* said)
solve /sɒlv/ solve (a problem) *n:* solution
spell /spel/
tell /tel/ (*pt, pp* told) tell sb (sth/that); tell sb (about sth; tell sth to sb
think /θɪŋk/ (*pt, pp* thought) think about (sth/sb)
try /traɪ/ (*pt, pp* tried) try to (do sth.)
understand /ˌʌndə'stænd/ (*pt, pp* understood) understand sb/sth
win /wɪn/ (*pt, pp* won) win sth; win a prize/competition

Adjectives

clear /klɪə(r)/
cooperative /kəʊ'ɒpərətɪv/ *opp:* uncooperative
different /'dɪfrənt/ *opp:* the same
fictional /'fɪkʃənl/
frustrated /frʌ'streɪtɪd/ feel frustrated with sth/sb; feel frustrated about sth.
generous /'dʒenərəs/
good fun /ˌɡʊd 'fʌn/
great /ɡreɪt/
hard-working /ˌhɑːd 'wɜːkɪŋ/ *opp:* lazy
honest /'ɒnɪst/
intelligent /ɪn'telɪdʒənt/ *opp:* unintelligent
interesting /'ɪntrəstɪŋ/ *opp:* uninteresting
lazy /'leɪzi/ (lazier; laziest)
magic /'mædʒɪk/
moody /'muːdi/
nervous /'nɜːvəs/
real /'riːəl/ *opp:* unreal
selfish /'selfɪʃ/ *opp:* unselfish
shy /ʃaɪ/ (shier; shiest)
special /'speʃl/
sporty /spɔːti/
sympathetic /ˌsɪmpə'θetɪk/ *opp:* unsympathetic
twin /twɪn/
unfriendly /ʌn'frendli/ *opp:* friendly

Adverbs

carefully /'keəfəli/ *adj:* careful

Phrasal verbs

give up (pt, gave; pp given) give (sth) up
go on (pt went; pp gone) go on doing sth

Unit 2

Nouns

acrobat /'ækrəʊbæt/
actress /'æktrɪs/
advice /əd'vaɪs/ give sb advice about sth; *v:* advise
ankle /'æŋkl/
arts /ɑːts/
audience /'ɔːdiəns/
choir /'kwaɪə(r)/
chorister /'kɒrɪstə(r)/
circus /'sɜːkəs/ (*pl* circuses)
contortionist /kən'tɔːʃənɪst/
earrings /'ɪərɪŋz/
interview /'ɪntəvjuː/ interview sb about sth; *v:* interview
jewellery /'dʒuːəlri/
juggler /'dʒʌɡlə(r)/
line /laɪn/ learn (your) lines for sth
move /muːv/
musical /'mjuːzɪkl/ *adj:* musical
neck /nek/
necklace /'nekləs/
orchestra /'ɔːkɪstrə/ play in an orchestra
parent /'peərənt/
performance /pə'fɔːməns/ give a performance; *v:* performance
piece /piːs/ a piece of sth
play /pleɪ/ *v:* play
present /'prezənt/ *v:* present
production /prə'dʌkʃn/ *v:* produce
reporter /rɪpɔːtə(r)/ *v:* report
singer /'sɪŋə(r)/ *v:* sing
sleeve /sliːv/
stage /steɪdʒ/ be on stage
string /strɪŋ/
suit /suːt/
term /tɜːm/
theatre /'θɪətə(r)/
tie /taɪ/
tracksuit /'træksuːt/
voice /vɔɪs/
weather /'weðə(r)/
wood /wʊd/

Verbs

act /ækt/ *n:* act
control /kən'trəʊl/
cover /'kʌvə(r)/
find /faɪnd/ (*pt, pp* found)
fly /flaɪ/ (*pt* flew; *pp* flown)
happen /'hæpən/
jog /dʒɒɡ/

move /muːv/ n: move
perform /pəˈfɔːm/ n: performance
prefer /prɪˈfɜː(r)/
prepare /prɪˈpeə(r)/ adj: prepared
record /rɪˈkɔːd/ n: record
rehearse /rɪˈhɜːs/ n: rehearsal
remember /rɪˈmembə(r)/
sound /saʊnd/ n: sound
wear /weə(r)/ (pt wore; pp worn)

Phrasal verbs

get changed   get changed (into sth)
put on   put sth on

Adjectives

determined /dɪˈtɜːmɪnd/ determined to do sth
except for /ɪkˈsept fɔː/
extra-curricular /ˌekstrə kʌˈrɪkjələ(r)/
famous /ˈfeɪməs/ famous for (doing) sth; n: fame
flexible /ˈfleksɪbl/ opp: inflexible
incredible /ɪnˈkredɪbl/ opp: credible
lucky /ˈlʌki/ (luckier; luckiest); opp: unlucky; n: luck
normal /ˈnɔːml/ opp: abnormal
prepared /prəˈpeəd/ unprepared; n: preparation; v: prepare
quick /kwɪk/ opp: slow
talented /ˈtæləntɪd/ talented at (doing) sth; n: talent
traditional /trəˈdɪʃənl/ opp: modern; n: tradition
typical /ˈtɪpɪkl/ typical of sth/sb
worried /ˈwʌrid/ n: worry; v: worry

Adverbs

obviously /ˈɒbviəsli/ adjective: obvious
usually /ˈjuːʒəli/ adjective: usual

Unit 3

Nouns

activity /ækˈtɪvəti/ adj: active
advert /ˈædvɜːt/ place an advert in a newspaper; v: advertise
article /ˈɑːtɪkl/ write an article on sth
businessman /ˈbɪznɪsmən/ (pl businessmen)
cartoon /kɑːˈtuːn/
celebrity /səˈlebrɪti/ (pl celebrities)
channel /ˈtʃænəl/
comedy programme /ˈkɒmədi ˌprəʊɡræm/
competition /ˌkɒmpəˈtɪʃn/ take part in a competition; v: compete
conclusion /kənˈkluːʒn/ v: conclude
contact /ˈkɒntækt/ v: contact
contestant /kənˈtestənt/
continent /ˈkɒntɪnənt/
cookery programme /ˈkʊkəri ˌprəʊɡræm/

current affairs /ˌkʌrənt əˈfeəz/
date /deɪt/
desert /ˈdezət/ adj: deserted
detective /dɪˈtektɪv/
discount /ˈdɪskaʊnt/
documentary /ˌdɒkjʊˈmentri/ (pl documentaries)
edition /ɪˈdɪʃn/
experience /ɪkˈspɪəriəns/ experience sth; adj: experienced
film /fɪlm/ v: film
introduction /ˌɪntrəˈdʌkʃn/ v: introduce
jungle /ˈdʒʌŋɡl/
market /ˈmɑːkɪt/
nationality /ˌnæʃəˈnæləti/ (pl nationalities); adj: national
news /njuːz/
personality /ˌpɜːsəˈnæləti/ (pl personalities)
place /pleɪs/
prediction /prəˈdɪkʃn/ v: predict
product /ˈprɒdʌkt/ v: produce
programme /ˈprəʊɡræm/ v: programme
quiz show /ˈkwɪz ˌʃəʊ/
reality /riˈæləti/ (pl realities) adj: real
report /rɪˈpɔːt/ v: report
snowboarding /ˈsnəʊbɔːdɪŋ/ v: snowboard
soap /səʊp/
survivor /səˈvaɪvə/ v: survive
technology /tekˈnɒlədʒi/ (pl technologies)
tourist /ˈtʊərɪst/ v: tour
weather forecast /ˈweðə ˌfɔːkɑːst/

Verbs

arrive /əˈraɪv/
choose /tʃuːz/ (pt, chose; pp chosen) n: choice
communicate /kəˈmjuːnɪkeɪt/ communicate with sb; n: communication
compare /kəmˈpeə(r)/
imagine /ɪˈmædʒɪn/ n: imagination
invent /ɪnˈvent/ n: invention
laugh /lɑːf/ laugh at/because of sth
must /mʌst/ (pt, have/had to)
phone /fəʊn/
spend /spend/ (pt, pp spent)
switch /swɪtʃ/ switch sth on/off

Adjectives

angry /ˈæŋɡri/ (angrier; angriest)
astonishing /əˈstɒnɪʃɪŋ/
awful /ˈɔːfl/
bad /bæd/ (worse; worst) opp: good
brilliant /ˈbrɪliənt/
cheap /tʃiːp/ opp: expensive
clean /kliːn/ opp: dirty
cool /kuːl/

dangerous /ˈdeɪndʒərəs/ *n:* danger
delicious /dɪˈlɪʃəs/
expensive /ɪkˈspensɪv/ *opp:* cheap
fantastic /fænˈtæstɪk/
fascinating /ˈfæsɪneɪtɪŋ/ *opp:* boring
fictitious /fɪkˈtɪʃəs/ *n:* fiction
friendly /ˈfrendli/ (friendlier; friendliest); *opp:* unfriendly
funny /ˈfʌni/ (funnier; funniest)
good /ɡʊd/ (better; best) *opp:* bad
great /ɡreɪt/
healthy /ˈhelθi/ *n:* health
hilarious /hɪˈleəriəs/
horrible /ˈhɒrəbl/
local /ˈləʊkl/
modern /ˈmɒdn/ *opp:* old fashioned
negative /ˈneɡətɪv/ *opp:* positive
possible /ˈpɒsəbl/ *opp:* impossible
pretty /ˈprɪti/ (prettier; prettiest)
romantic /rəʊˈmæntɪk/ *n:* romance
surprising /səˈpraɪzɪŋ/ *n:* surprise
terrible /ˈterəbl/
terrifying /ˈterɪfaɪɪŋ/
thin /θɪn/ (thinner; thinnest) *opp:* fat
weekly /ˈwiːkli/
wonderful /ˈwʌndəfl/

Adverbs

especially /ɪˈspeʃəli/ *adj:* special
extremely /ɪkˈstriːmli/ *adj:* extreme
really /ˈriːəli/ *adj:* real

Unit 4

Nouns

assistant /əˈsɪstənt/ assist sb to do sth; *v:* assist
astronaut /ˈæstrənɔːt/
boarding card /ˈbɔːdɪŋ kɑːd/
boomerang /ˈbuːməræŋ/
bridge /ˈbrɪdʒ/
building /ˈbɪldɪŋ/
celebration /seləˈbreɪʃən/ celebrate (doing) sth; *v:* celebrate
desert /ˈdezət/
disaster /dɪˈzɑːstə(r)/
escalator /ˈeskəleɪtə(r)/
event /ɪˈvent/ go to/ attend an event
fire /ˈfaɪə(r)/
flight attendant /ˈflaɪt əˈtendənt/
fraud /frɔːd/ *v:* commit fraud
marathon /ˈmærəθən/ run/take part in (a) marathon
moment /ˈməʊmənt/
moon /muːn/
passenger /ˈpæsɪndʒə(r)/ be a passenger on sth

passport /ˈpɑːspɔːt/
passport control /ˈpɑːspɔːt kənˈtrəʊl/
plane /pleɪn/
project /ˈprɒdʒekt/
route /ruːt/
skin /skɪn/
sky /skaɪ/
snake /sneɪk/
souvenir /suːvəˈnɪə(r)/
space /speɪs/
spaceship /ˈspeɪs ʃɪp/
spear /spɪə(r)/ *v:* spear
stair /steə(r)/
star /stɑː(r)/ *v:* star
studio /ˈstjuːdiəʊ/
swimming costume /ˈswɪmɪŋ kɒstjuːm/
ticket /ˈtɪkɪt/ buy a ticket for sth
tradition /trəˈdɪʃn/ *adj:* traditional

Verbs

answer /ˈɑːnsə(r)/ *n:* answer
break /breɪk/ *adj:* broken
bring /brɪŋ/ bring sth somewhere/to sb (*pt, pp* brought)
catch /kætʃ/ (*pt, pp* caught) *n:* catch
celebrate /ˈselɪbreɪt/ *n:* celebration
disappear /dɪsəˈpɪə(r)/ disappear from somewhere
drop /drɒp/
forget /fəˈɡet/ (*pt* forgot; *pp* forgotten) forget to do sth
hurry /ˈhʌri/ (*pt, pp* hurried); be in a hurry to (do sth/ get somewhere) *n:* hurry
land /lænd/
laugh /lɑːf/ laugh at sth/sb; *n:* laughter
lose /luːz/ (*pt, pp* lost) *adj:* lost
meet /miːt/ (*pt, pp* met)
notice /ˈnəʊtɪs/ *n:* notice
put /pʊt/ (*pt, pp* put)
return /rɪˈtɜːn/ return from somewhere
took /tʊk/ (*pt* took *pp* taken)
travel /ˈtrævl/ *n:* travel
want /wɒnt/

Phrasal verbs

come back (from) come back (from somewhere)
get off get off sth
get on get on (to) sth
set out to set out to do sth/go somewhere
take off (a) plane takes off
took down take sb down to a place

Adjectives

dark /dɑːk/ *opp:* light
late /leɪt/ *opp:* early
lost /lɒst/ *opp:* found
strange /streɪndʒ/ *opp:* normal
unusual /ʌnˈjuːʒuəl/ *opp:* usual

Prepositions of movement

across /əˈkrɒs/
down /daʊn/ *opp:* up
over /ˈəʊvə(r)/ *opp:* under
through /θruː/
under /ˈʌndə(r)/ *opp:* over
up /ʌp/ *opp:* down

Unit 5

Nouns

accident /ˈæksɪdənt/ *adj:* accidental
art gallery /ˈɑːt gæləri/ (*pl* art galleries)
beach /biːtʃ/
car park /ˈkɑː pɑːk/
cinema /ˈsɪnəmə/
community /kəˈmjuːnəti/ (*pl* communities)
condition /kənˈdɪʃn/
criminal /ˈkrɪmɪnl/
culture /ˈkʌltʃə(r)/ *adj:* cultural
danger /ˈdeɪndʒə(r)/ be in danger from sth/sb; *adj:* dangerous
factory /ˈfæktri/ (*pl* factories)
firefighter /ˈfaɪəfaɪtə(r)/
government /ˈgʌvənmənt/
gunfighter /ˈgʌnfaɪtə(r)/
hero /ˈhɪərəʊ/ (*pl* heroes)
human /ˈhjuːmən/
image /ˈɪmɪdʒ/
legend /ˈledʒənd/
librarian /laɪˈbreəriən/
library /ˈlaɪbrəri/ (*pl* libraries)
mayor /ˈmeə(r)/
organisation /ˌɔːgənaɪˈzeɪʃn/ *v:* organise
orphan /ˈɔːfn/
orphanage /ˈɔːfənɪdʒ/
policeman /pəˈliːsmən/ (*pl* policemen)
president /ˈprezɪdənt/
pupil /ˈpjuːpl/
ranch /ˈrɑːntʃ/ (*pl* ranches)
sheriff /ˈʃerɪf/
situation /ˌsɪtʃuˈeɪʃn/
slavery /ˈsleɪvəri/
spider /ˈspaɪdə(r)/
stadium /ˈsteɪdiəm/
superhero /ˈsuːpəhɪərəʊ/ (*pl* superheroes)

tail /teɪl/
town hall /ˌtaʊnˈhɔːl/
traveller /ˈtrævələ(r)/ *v:* travel
village /ˈvɪlɪdʒ/
war /wɔː(r)/
worker /ˈwɜːkə(r)/ *v:* work

Verbs

appear /əˈpɪə(r)/ *n:* appearance
attack /əˈtæk/ *n:* attack
bite /baɪt/ (*pt* bit; *pp* bitten)
borrow /ˈbɒrəʊ/ borrow sth from sb
build /bɪld/ (*pt, pp* built)
catch /kætʃ/ (*pt, pp* caught)
collect /kəˈlekt/ *n:* collection
continue /kənˈtɪnjuː/ continue to (do sth)
create /kriˈeɪt/ create sth *adj:* creative
destroy /dɪˈstrɔɪ/ *adj:* destroyed
die /daɪ/ (*pt, pp* died)
follow /ˈfɒləʊ/
hear /hɪə(r)/ (*pt, pp* heard)
help /help/ help sb (to do sth) *n:* help
introduce /ˌɪntrəˈdjuːs/ introduce sb/sth to sb; *n:* introduction
kill /kɪl/ *n:* killer
protect /prəˈtekt/ protect sb/sth from sb/sth; *adj:* protected
pull /pʊl/ (*pt, pp* pull)
realise /ˈriːəlaɪz/ realise sth
rob /rɒb/ *n:* robbery
stop /stɒp/ stop doing sth
surf /sɜːf/
survive /səˈvaɪv/
swim /swɪm/ (*pt* swam; *pp* swum)
use /juːz/ (*pt, pp* used)
write /raɪt/ (*pt* wrote; *pp* written)

Phrasal verbs

get up get up from sth
go down go down somewhere
look after look after sb

Adjectives

bored /bɔːd/ bored (with sth)
awful /ˈɔːfl/
boring /ˈbɔːrɪŋ/
brave /breɪv/
determined /dɪˈtɜːmɪnd/ determined to do sth
disabled /dɪsˈeɪbld/
frightened /ˈfraɪtnd/ frightened of sth/sb
frightening /ˈfraɪtnɪŋ/
ill /ɪl/ *opp:* well
international /ˌɪntəˈnæʃnəl/ *opp:* national
later /ˈleɪtə(r)/ *opp:* earlier

native /ˈneɪtɪv/
nearby /nɪəˈbaɪ/ *opp:* far away
perfect /ˈpɜːfekt/ *opp:* imperfect
poor /pɔː(r)/ *opp:* rich
radioactive /reɪdɪəʊˈæktɪv/
rich /rɪtʃ/ *opp:* poor
surprised /səˈpraɪzd/ feel surprised at/about sth
surprising /səˈpraɪzɪŋ/ sth is surprising
terrible /ˈterəbl/
well /wel/ *opp:* ill
well-known /ˌwelˈnəʊn/
wild /waɪld/
worrying /ˈwʌriɪŋ/

Adverbs

probably /ˈprɒbəbli/ *adj:* probable

Prepositions

until /ənˈtɪl/

Unit 6

Nouns

accident /ˈæksɪdənt/ *adj:* accidental
bear /beə(r)/
boat /bəʊt/
chance /ˈtʃɑːns/ have a chance to do sth
damage /ˈdæmɪdʒ/ *v:* damage; *adj:* damaged
drought /draʊt/ suffer from drought
earthquake /ˈɜːθkweɪk/
equator /ɪˈkweɪtə(r)/
experience /ɪkˈspɪərɪəns/ *v:* experience; *adj:* experienced
explosion /ɪkˈspləʊʒn/ *v:* explode
flood /flʌd/ *v:* flood
floor /flɔː(r)/
forest /ˈfɒrɪst/
hurricane /ˈhʌrɪkən/
journey /ˈdʒɜːni/ make a journey to somewhere
lightning /ˈlaɪtnɪŋ/
ocean /əʊʃn/
roof /ruːf/
storm /stɔːm/ *adj:* stormy
tectonic plate /tekˈtɒnɪk pleɪt/
tent /tent/
thunder /ˈθʌndə(r)/
tornado /tɔːˈneɪdəʊ/ (*pl* tornadoes)
tourist /ˈtʊərɪst/
tsunami wave /tsuːˈnɑːmi ˌweɪv/
type /taɪp/
volcano /vɒlˈkeɪnəʊ/ (*pl* volcanoes)

Verbs

cause /kɔːz/ cause sth to happen; *n:* cause
crash /kræʃ/ *n:* crash
cycle /ˈsaɪkl/
destroy /dɪˈstrɔɪ/ destroy sth
disappear /dɪsəˈpɪə/ *n:* disappearance
discover /dɪsˈkʌvə(r)/ *n:* discovery
drop /drɒp/
dry /draɪ/
explain /ɪkˈspleɪn/ explain sth to sb; exlain about sth; *n:* explanation
fall /fɔːl/ (*pt* fell; *pp* fallen) *n:* fall
form /fɔːm/
happen /ˈhæpən/
pass /pɑːs/ pass an exam
rain /reɪn/ *n:* rain
recognise /ˈrekəgnaɪz/
remember /rɪˈmembə(r)/ remember to do sth; remember doing sth
ski /skiː/ *n:* ski
stay /steɪ/
survive /səˈvaɪv/ *n:* survival
throw /θrəʊ/ (pt threw; pp thrown)
understand /ʌndəˈstænd/ *n:* understanding
worry /ˈwʌri/ *n:* worry

Phrasal verbs

go across   go across sth
go out with   go out with sb
set off   set off to do sth

Adjectives

anxious /ˈæŋkʃəs/
ashamed /əˈʃeɪmd/ *opp:* unashamed
desperate /ˈdesprət/
enthusiastic /ɪnθjuːziˈæstɪk/ *opp:* unenthusiastic
extreme /ɪkˈstriːm/
glad /glæd/ (gladder; gladdest)
grateful /ˈgreɪtfl/ *opp:* ungrateful
proud /praʊd/
relaxed /rɪˈlækst/ *opp:* tense
safe /seɪf/ *opp:* unsafe
tense /tens/ *opp:* relaxed
tired /taɪəd/
uninterested /ʌnˈɪntrəstɪd/ *opp:* interested
upset /ʌpˈset/

Adverbs

firstly /ˈfɜːstli/ *adj:* first
suddenly /ˈsʌdnli/ *adj:* sudden

Unit 7

Nouns

aunt /ɑːnt/
barbecue /ˈbɑːbɪkjuː/ v: barbecue
brat /bræt/
camp /kæmp/ v: camp
coach /kəʊtʃ/ (pl coaches) v: coach
downtown /ˈdaʊnˈtaʊn/ go downtown (US)
family /ˈfæmli/ (pl families)
father-in-law /ˈfɑːðərɪnlɔː/
ferris wheel /ˈferɪs wiːl/
firework display /ˈfaɪəwɜːk ˌdɪspleɪ/
flag /flæg/
foot /fʊt/ (pl feet)
football /ˈfʊtbɔːl/ play football against sb (US soccer)
free fall /ˈfriː ˌfɔːl/ v: free fall
grandfather /ˈgrænfɑːðə(r)/
grandmother /ˈgrænmʌðə(r)/
husband /ˈhʌzbənd/
mistake /mɪˈsteɪk/ adj: mistaken
mother-in-law /ˈmʌðərɪnlɔː/
nephew /ˈnefjuː/
niece /niːs/
parade /pəˈreɪd/ take part in a parade; v: parade
Pharaoh /ˈfeərəʊ/ (pl Pharoahs)
picnic /ˈpɪknɪk/ have a picnic somewhere; v: picnic
ride /raɪd/ v: ride
roller coaster /ˈrəʊlə(r) ˌkəʊstə(r)/
show /ʃəʊ/ v: show
soccer /ˈsɒkə(r)/ (UK football)
teenager /ˈtiːneɪdʒə(r)/
Thanksgiving /ˈθæŋks ˌgɪvɪŋ/ (US)
theme park /ˈθiːm ˌpɑːk/
uncle /ˈʌŋkl/
washing up /wɒʃɪŋ ˈʌp/ do the washing up; v: wash up
water flume /ˈwɔːtə ˌfluːm/
wife /waɪf/ (pl wives)

Verbs

behave /bɪˈheɪv/ n: behaviour
celebrate /ˈselɪbreɪt/ celebrate sth; n: celebration
carry /ˈkæri/ (pt, pp carried)
hope /həʊp/ hope sth will happen; hope to do sth; n: hope

Adjectives

crazy /ˈkreɪzi/ (crazier; craziest)
special /ˈspeʃl/

Adverbs

well /wel/
traditionally /trəˈdɪʃənəli/ adj: traditional

Unit 8

Nouns

animal /ˈænɪml/
bottle /ˈbɒtl/
campaign /kæmˈpeɪn/ campaign for/against sth; v: campaign
charity /ˈtʃærəti/ donate (money) to charity; (pl charities) adj: charitable
demonstration /demənˈstreɪʃn/ go on a demonstration
destruction /dɪˈstrʌkʃn/ v: destroy
director /daɪˈrektə(r)/ v: direct
environment /ɪnˈvaɪrənmənt/ adj: environmental
glass /glɑːs/
guide /gaɪd/ v: guide
information pack /ɪnfəˈmeɪʃn ˌpæk/
material /məˈtɪəriəl/
medicine /ˈmedsn/
packaging /ˈpækɪdʒɪŋ/ v: package
part /pɑːt/ (a) part of sth
petition /pəˈtɪʃn/ sign a petition
planet /ˈplænɪt/
plant /plɑːnt/ v: plant
plastic /ˈplæstɪk/ adj: plastic
pollution /pəˈluːʃn/ v: pollute
rainforest /ˈreɪnfɒrɪst/
reservation /rezəˈveɪʃn/
resource /rɪˈzɔːs/ adj: resourceful
rubbish /ˈrʌbɪʃ/
tiger /ˈtaɪgə(r)/
tradition /trəˈdɪʃn/ adj: traditional
zoology /zəʊˈɒlədʒi/

Verbs

change /tʃeɪndʒ/ n: change; adj: changed
collect /kəˈlekt/ n: collection
enter /ˈentə(r)/
improve /ɪmˈpruːv/ n: improvement; adj: improved
organise /ˈɔːgənaɪz/ adj: organised
protect /prəˈtekt/ protect sth/sb from sth/sb; n: protection; adj: protected
recognise /ˈrekəgnaɪz/
recycle /riːˈsaɪkl/ n: recycling; adj: recycled
save /seɪv/ save sth/sb from sth/sb
sign /saɪn/ n: signature
transform /trænsˈfɔːm/ transform sth into sth; n: transformation
wait /weɪt/ wait for sb/sth; wait for sth to happen; n: wait
waste /weɪst/ n: waste

Adjectives

difficult /ˈdɪfɪkəlt/ difficult to do sth *opp:* easy
green /griːn/
harmless /ˈhɑːmləs/ *opp:* harmful
homemade /ˈhəʊmˌmeɪd/
less /les/ *opp:* more
natural /ˈnætʃrəl/ *opp:* unnatural
necessary /ˈnesəsəri/ necessary to do sth; *opp:* unnecessary
plastic /ˈplæstɪk/
recycled /riːˈsaɪkld/
sad /sæd/ (sadder; saddest) *opp:* happy

Adverbs

approximately /əˈprɒksɪmətli/ *adj:* approximate

Phrasal verbs

leave on leave sth on
throw away throw sth away

Verbs

mention /ˈmenʃən/ mention sth to sb (about sth); *n:* mention
paint /peɪnt/ *n:* paint
search /sɜːtʃ/ search for sth; *n:* search

Adjectives

close /kləʊz/ be close to sth/sb; *opp:* far
gold /gəʊld/
junior /ˈdʒuːnɪə/ *opp:* senior
multiplex /ˈmʌltɪˌpleks/
positive /ˈpɒzɪtɪv/ be positive about sth; *opp:* negative
recent /ˈriːsnt/
spare /speə(r)/
tidy /ˈtaɪdi/ (tidier; tidiest) *opp:* untidy
untidy /ʌnˈtaɪdi/ (untidier; untidiest); *opp:* tidy

Adverbs

never /ˈnevə(r)/

Unit 9

Nouns

adventure /ədˈventʃə(r)/ have an adventure
agent /ˈeɪdʒənt/
bully /ˈbʊli/ (*pl* bullies); *v:* bully
championship /ˈtʃæmpiənʃɪp/
classmate /ˈklɑːsmeɪt/
cottage /ˈkɒtɪdʒ/
desk /desk/
difference /ˈdɪfrəns/ *adj:* different
exercise book /ˈeksəsaɪz ˌbʊk/
farm /fɑːm/ *v:* farm
fast food /ˈfɑːst ˈfuːd/
field /fiːld/
footpath /ˈfʊtpɑːθ/
furniture /ˈfɜːnɪtʃə(r)/
gun /gʌn/
hairstyle /ˈheəstaɪl/
hill /hɪl/
locker /ˈlɒkə(r)/ *v:* lock; *adj:* locked
medal /ˈmedl/ win a medal for (doing) sth
pocket money /ˈpɒkɪt ˌmʌni/ get pocket money
record /ˈrekɔːd/ keep a record of sth; *v:* record
rucksack /ˈrʌksæk/
rule /ruːl/ *v:* rule; *adj:* ruled
security man /səˈkjʊərəti ˌmæn/
stream /striːm/
text book /ˈtekst ˌbʊk/
valley /ˈvæli/
village /ˈvɪlɪdʒ/
woods /wʊdz/

Irregular verbs

base form	past simple	past participle	base form	past simple	past participle
be	was / were	been	lend	lent	lent
beat	beat	beaten	let	let	let
become	became	become	lie	lay	lain
begin	began	begun	lie	lied	lied
bend	bent	bent	lose	lost	lost
bet	bet	bet	make	made	made
bite	bit	bitten	mean	meant	meant
bleed	bled	bled	meet	met	met
blow	blew	blown	pay	paid	paid
break	broke	broken	put	put	put
bring	brought	brought	read	read	read
build	built	built	ride	rode	ridden
burn	burned, burnt	burned, burnt	ring	rang	rung
buy	bought	bought	rise	rose	risen
catch	caught	caught	run	ran	run
choose	chose	chosen	say	said	said
come	came	come	see	saw	seen
cost	cost	cost	sell	sold	sold
cut	cut	cut	send	sent	sent
dig	dug	dug	shake	shook	shaken
do	did	done	shine	shone	shone
draw	drew	drawn	shoot	shot	shot
dream	dreamed, dreamt	dreamed, dreamt	show	showed	shown
drink	drank	drunk	shut	shut	shut
drive	drove	driven	sing	sang	sung
eat	ate	eaten	sit	sat	sat
fall	fell	fallen	sleep	slept	slept
feed	fed	fed	smell	smelt	smelt
feel	felt	felt	speak	spoke	spoken
fight	fought	fought	spell	spelt	spelt
find	found	found	spend	spent	spent
fly	flew	flown	spill	spilt	spilt
forget	forgot	forgotten	spoil	spoilt	spoilt
forgive	forgave	forgiven	spread	spread	spread
get	got	got	stand	stood	stood
give	gave	given	steal	stole	stolen
go	went	been / gone	sweep	swept	swept
grow	grew	grown	swim	swam	swum
hang	hung	hung	swing	swung	swung
have	had	had	take	took	taken
hear	heard	heard	teach	taught	taught
hit	hit	hit	tear	tore	torn
hold	held	held	tell	told	told
hurt	hurt	hurt	think	thought	thought
keep	kept	kept	throw	threw	thrown
know	knew	known	understand	understood	understood
lead	led	led	wear	wore	worn
learn	learnt, learned	learnt, learned	win	won	won
leave	left	left	write	wrote	written

UNIVERSITY PRESS

Great Clarendon Street, Oxford OX2 6DP

Oxford University Press is a department of the University of Oxford.
It furthers the University's objective of excellence in research, scholarship,
and education by publishing worldwide in

Oxford New York

Auckland Cape Town Dar es Salaam Hong Kong Karachi
Kuala Lumpur Madrid Melbourne Mexico City Nairobi
New Delhi Shanghai Taipei Toronto

With offices in

Argentina Austria Brazil Chile Czech Republic France Greece
Guatemala Hungary Italy Japan Poland Portugal Singapore
South Korea Switzerland Thailand Turkey Ukraine Vietnam

OXFORD and OXFORD ENGLISH are registered trade marks of
Oxford University Press in the UK and in certain other countries

© Oxford University Press 2007

ISBN-13: 978 0 19 412900 8

Printed in China

ACKNOWLEDGEMENTS

The author would like to thank everyone who has helped in the creation of
this book, especially the staff of Oxford University Press, Pippa Mayfield, Lara
Storton and Julia Pons Vidal.

Designed by: Rob Hancock Design Ltd.

Researched photography and art editing by: G. Metcalfe

We would like to thank the following for their permission to reproduce photographs:
Alamy Images pp13 (Volleyball Team/Aflo Foto Agency), 68 (Water splash/Roy
Woodward), 70 (mountain biking/Nick Gregory), 71 (Classic cars, USA/Visions
of America, LLC/Joe Sohm), 85 (Family on a boat ride/Steve Bly), 92 (three
teenage girls /Jennie Hart); The British Film Institute p. 26 (*The Simpsons*);
Corbis pp 6 (boy), 14 (1, 3, 7, 8, 10), 18 (Smiling Young Woman Looking
Through Curtain/zefa/Schultheiss Productions), 18 (rehearsal, classroom,
musicians), 20 (science lesson, rugby, boy portrait), 21 (both), 23 (performer
from the Chinese National Circus/Juan Medina/Reuters), 23 (Le cirque du
soleil/Steff), 23 (juggler), 28 (computers), 30 (Will Smith), 31 (watching TV),
32 (both), 35 (football), 36 (girl writing), 37 (TV screens), 40, 46, 48 (all), 49, 52
(Mahatma Gandhi/Hulton-Deutsch Collection), 62, 65 (storm), 66 (hiking), 68
(rollercoaster), 71 (meal), 75 (3, 5), 76, 78, 79 (lion, elephant), 82 (classroom),
88, 90 (all), 91 (car), 92 (teacher, couple), 93 (all); Getty Images pp 14 (6, 9), 15
(Boys sitting on curb/Riser), 16 (all), 20 (choir, ice cream), 26 (Herkat
Sufian/AFP/Karim Jaafar), 29 (man with camera), 31 (computer games,
basketball), 34 (all), 37 (cinema), 43, 51 (all), 60, 66 (Rick), 67 (Nina), 70
(sailing), 70 (Man with teenage boys at campsite/The Image Bank/Yellow Dog
Productions), 71 (fireworks), 72 (safari, London), 74 (all), 75 (1, 2, 4), 78 (all
except 1), 79 (girl, rhino), 82 (cycling, shopping, science), 87 (friends,
Guggenheim), 91 (riding); Kobal Collection pp. 19, 50 (all), 52 (Robin Hood,
Cleopatra); OUP pp68 (Ferris wheel/Photodisc), 72 (Tropical Beach/Photodisc);
PunchStock pp6 (Teenage girl talking on cell phone/Blend Images), 10 (boy
smiling/IT Stock), 14 (Boys playing videogames/Comstock), 14 (Hispanic
family camping/Blend Images), 14 (Gymnast/PhotoAlto), 66 (Bride standing in
garden/Photodisc); Rex Features p70 (children rock climbing/David Cole), 78
(charity collecting); Robert Harding pp. 26 (Paula, Mamadou, Keiko, Yolanda),
44 (all), 87 (bridge); RTVE p. 26 (*Informe Semanal* still); Topfoto pp. 8 (Henley),
52 (Maradona, Miguel Indurain), 54, 57, 59.

Illustrations by: Adrian Barclay p. 4 ('Britain 1901-2000' book cover); Oliver
Hutton pp. 23, 43, 59, 79; Sophie Joyce pp. 12, 19, 22, 39, 42, 58, 83, 86; Rui
Ricardo/Folio London pp. 4, 5, 7, 8 (left hand column), 9; Lola and
Rosanas/Folio London pp. 30, 38, 41, 56, 84.